Deschutes
Public Library

D0407798

VALEDICTORIANS AT THE GATE

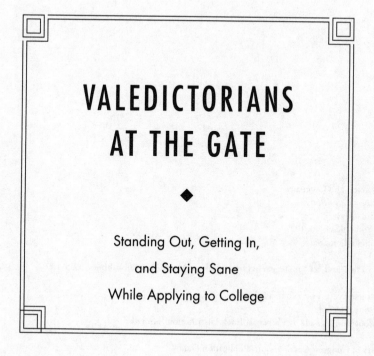

VALEDICTORIANS
AT THE GATE

◆

Standing Out, Getting In,
and Staying Sane
While Applying to College

Becky Munsterer Sabky

Henry Holt and Company

New York

Henry Holt and Company
Publishers since 1866
120 Broadway
New York, New York 10271
www.henryholt.com

Henry Holt® and Ⓗ® are registered trademarks of Macmillan Publishing Group, LLC.

Copyright © 2021 by Rebecca Sabky
All rights reserved.
Distributed in Canada by Raincoast Book Distribution Limited

Library of Congress Cataloging-in-Publication Data

Names: Sabky, Rebecca Munsterer, 1978– author.
Title: Valedictorians at the gate : standing out, getting in, and staying sane while applying
    to college / Becky Munsterer Sabky.
Description: First edition. | New York : Henry Holt and Company, [2021] | Includes
    bibliographical references.
Identifiers: LCCN 2020047926 (print) | LCCN 2020047927 (ebook) |
    ISBN 9781250619037 (hardcover) | ISBN 9781250619044 (ebook)
Subjects: LCSH: College choice—United States. | Universities and colleges—
    United States—Admission.
Classification: LCC LB2350.5 .S23 2021 (print) | LCC LB2350.5 (ebook) |
    DDC 378.1/610973—dc23
LC record available at https://lccn.loc.gov/2020047926
LC ebook record available at https://lccn.loc.gov/2020047927

Our books may be purchased in bulk for promotional, educational, or business use. Please contact
your local bookseller or the Macmillan Corporate and Premium Sales Department at (800) 221-7945,
extension 5442, or by e-mail at MacmillanSpecialMarkets@macmillan.com.

First Edition 2021

Designed by Karen Minster

Printed in the United States of America

10 9 8 7 6 5 4 3 2 1

For Debbie and
Jerry Munsterer

Contents

SPECIAL CONSIDERATIONS

POSTDECISION

PREFACE

In 1997, I was denied admission to Dartmouth College. It was my first-choice school. I received the bad news from a dean of admissions I would curse for a week.

The denial was senseless. I *belonged* at Dartmouth. I was near the top of my class, was president of the National Honor Society, and had competed in the Junior Olympics for alpine skiing. My teeth were straight, my vocabulary was decent, and I wore conservative L.L.Bean sweaters designed for New England preps.

But something was wrong with me. Something wasn't good enough. I wasn't Dartmouth material.

I wasn't admitted to my second-, third-, or fourth-choice school either. (I spent the majority of April crying at the mailbox.) For someone who hadn't failed at much in my life, the rejections stung. I buried my Middlebury, Williams, and Bowdoin T-shirts far in the back of my closet, hoping I'd forget the schools that broke my heart.

Colby College was my fifth-choice school. It didn't have the Ivy stamp. It wasn't as highly ranked as Williams. But as I'd quickly learn, it did have an *amazing* creative writing department, a Rolodex of alumni happy to offer student summer internships, and perfectly crunchy onion rings. At Colby, I learned about Chaucer, microeconomics, and friendship. I used my creative writing skills to pen a few publishable newspaper columns (and to name dorm parties). I spent four years working hard as a student intern for the admissions office, which galvanized my love for all things recruitment. And life went on.

A few years later, a new application sat with the Dartmouth Admissions Office. After completing a two-year master's in the liberal studies program at Dartmouth, I decided to apply to work for the dean who had rejected me. I had two years of admissions experience at St. Lawrence University (a private liberal arts college in upstate New York), a graduate diploma, and a new set of L.L.Bean sweaters. Yet, after my first rejection, I wasn't sure I'd land the job, nor was I sure I should have even bothered with another application.

I'm glad I bothered. The same dean who denied my college application hired me to admit other college students. I'd be a senior assistant director of admissions with my own office, my own travel territory, and my own Dartmouth business card. I was handed the magic wand and tasked with recruiting, reviewing, and admitting a class of students from the many applicants. This Dartmouth College reject would now do the rejecting. The irony was palpable.

I loved working in the office. But it was only after I worked behind the scenes that I realized how misguided my original notion of college "worthiness" was. As a trained, experienced, and decisive admissions reviewer, I was voting on a student's *application,* not his person. My colleagues and I weren't qualified to make statements of value or character. While we could open the gate for around 10 percent of the applicants to Dartmouth, it didn't mean they were more "elite" than others in the pool. We were simply creating a class to fill the college's needs.

This book explores my personal experiences at the college over thirteen years as an Ivy League admissions officer. It's both narrative and prescriptive as I attempt to humanize the process and offer advice on how to survive the hullabaloo. It's filled with stories (both inspiring and head-scratching) and tips (e.g., the correct pronunciation of "Worcestershire" will wow a steak-loving alum during an interview). But most of all, it's a guide to keeping perspective while navigating a complex process.

There are a few things to note before reading.

1. **I've changed identifying details to protect those involved.**
Names, places, schools, and application specifics have been altered. Confidentiality is of highest concern to me, but I've done my best to preserve

the gist of my experiences. (So, if you believe you're the male chess champion from Connecticut who was denied from the college, I can assure you that the applicant was not male, did not play chess, and was not from Connecticut.)

2. I do not write about financial aid in this book.

I have never worked in financial aid. I'm not trained in the process. Dartmouth had a need-blind policy for American citizens, meaning that admissions officers were not to consider ability to pay tuition as part of their decision-making process. While I was never exposed to the financial aid records of our applicants with United States citizenship and don't feel qualified to comment on financial aid practices, I can't emphasize enough my concern about college affordability and accessibility. Net price is critical to college access, and I believe financial aid to be of utmost consideration when applying to and choosing colleges. I encourage every applicant, regardless of family income, to carefully research and consider financial aid offerings and policies. (And I beg students to pick up the phone and call a college's financial aid office if they have any doubts.)

3. I've worked as an admissions officer at two institutions: St. Lawrence University in Canton, New York, and Dartmouth College in Hanover, New Hampshire. I've admired (and still admire) them both.

St. Lawrence is my father's alma mater. He loved his experience there, and his enthusiasm rubbed off on me at an early age. I don't write much about my time there because I spent two years in an entry-level position, learning the ropes of what it meant to be an admissions officer while also learning how to "adult." (At SLU, I learned to never put a fork in a microwave, to always check the popcorn machine at the local bar for mice before taking a scoop, and to recruit tour guide volunteers with free pizza.) My time in the village of Canton, New York, confirmed my love for the profession (and my admiration for incredible colleagues), but most of my admissions career happened during my thirteen years at Dartmouth.

———————

Dartmouth College is an incredible institution. It provided me with remarkable professional growth and outstanding travel opportunities. (On recruitment trips, I saw the Jungle Room in Graceland, the Christ the Redeemer statue in Rio, and the canals of Venice.) I still live a few miles from the Dartmouth Green and call many former colleagues friends. I have nothing but admiration for Dartmouth's admissions office, its students, and its extended campus community.

But the obsession over getting into Dartmouth seemed all-consuming for many families. Most colleges admit the majority of students in their pools. Yet, in competitive college admissions markets, I witnessed many families who viewed admittance to top-ranked schools as a prize.

We need to help our students *apply* to college rather than *compete* for college. We need to remember that there's a school for everyone, and not everyone needs to attend any one school. We need to appreciate the path to the college gate, and not just celebrate the few who are passed through. And we must remind ourselves that admissions decisions aren't value statements; they're just business.

Twenty years later, I'm grateful to Dartmouth for sending me the thin envelope. It made me a more sympathetic admissions officer. (I kept the letter in the top drawer of my desk in case I took myself too seriously in the position.) It taught me a lesson about valuing open windows rather than obsessing about shut doors. It made me recognize that a person's talents, work ethic, abilities, and character don't change whether they are admitted to their first-choice institution or not. And it inspired me to want to help others gain perspective on an admissions process gone mad.

VALEDICTORIANS AT THE GATE

CHAPTER ONE

THE BIG PICTURE

"So, what *really* happens in there?"

It's a question I'm regularly asked when folks find out I was an admissions director. They want to know what happens behind closed doors. *"Do you actually read every application?" "Does the dean always have the final say?" "Do you ever just secretly flip a coin?"* (I've never been asked this question, but I know at least one parent was thinking it.)

The application process is not transparent. Admissions officers fiercely preserve and protect the privacy of their decisions. As a student applying to colleges I, too, was fiercely curious about what happened behind the scenes.

I had heard that admissions decision making was an art. I had heard it was a science. And some admissions counselors had publicly proclaimed it to be an "artsy science."

But after becoming an insider, I learned that the process is more of a business. An artsy-science-y business.

"Why would a student born in July be named October?" * a committee colleague commented while biting off a Twizzler head.

"Maybe that's when she was conceived," another colleague chimed in. "Kind of like when people name their kids after locations where they were conceived. Paris. Brooklyn."

---

* In this chapter, I share examples of how conversations about applicants *could have* progressed. As a reminder, I've changed all identifying details of applicants and their candidacies. (October and all other applicants are fictional.)

"Schenectady," another colleague muttered sarcastically.

It wasn't my first time at the admissions rodeo, but I was the rookie in the room. I had worked for two years at St. Lawrence University before joining the Dartmouth staff. At St. Lawrence, 60 percent of students were admitted. At Dartmouth, we were nearing the 10 percent mark.

I had been on the job for a few months, learning the ropes of reading. The process itself was straightforward (and similar to other processes at competitive institutions). Every application received at least two independent reads. (The regional admissions officer read the app first, summarizing and taking notes on the file.) Applications with stronger votes were sent for a dean's final read. Applications with fewer strong votes were sent for a director's third look. (Those whom the dean or director weren't ready to admit or deny were kicked to committee.)

In addition to learning how files were processed, I was trained how to read the applications. Nothing was out of the ordinary. *Record all grade trends from freshman to senior years. Summarize essays succinctly. Read U.S. citizens abroad in context of their school group.* I'd read about a couple dozen early decision applications on my own and was now sitting on the early decision committee. Reading applications had come naturally to me, but voting was a whole other story.

"What do you think, Becky?" the committee chair asked me.

"Maybe October is a family name," I said with a shrug.

"Not about the name, about her candidacy."

I liked October. She was a Latinx woman interested in science from a high school where Dartmouth historically didn't see many applications. "I see the admit."

"I don't," the Twizzler eater disagreed. "She's strong, certainly, but not a standout in the pool."

The committee chair nodded his head at the Twizzler eater. "Other thoughts?"

October's application spoke for itself. She was involved in gymnastics. She was an active school tutor. Her recommenders spoke to her engagement in the classroom. She was a very strong student with multiple interests.

"Then, let's take a vote," he continued. "Admit?"

I raised my hand.

"Defer?"

No hands raised.

"Deny?"

Four hands raised.

"The denies have it," the committee chair wrote as he scribbled down the 1–0–4 vote on a spreadsheet. "Next!"

As I looked around the room, I wondered if I'd ever be as confident in my votes as my colleagues. They were a mix of people who were young, old, skinny, chubby, Black, white, Native, gay, straight, left-handed, and pigeon-toed.* Some were Dartmouth alumni. Others had graduated from various other universities throughout the country. As much as they were likable, they were also intimidating. (They were NPR-listening, black-coffee-drinking folks. I was fonder of pop music and pumpkin spice lattes.)

Somehow these colleagues had figured out how to be discerning with their reviews. But in my individual application reading, I had voted to admit many more applications than I should have. Everyone struck me as deserving a spot in the class. In committee, I was committing the same crime.

"Now we have Reginald from Philadelphia, a white male, who is his local chess champion," the committee chair said between bites of Twizzlers.

"That's interesting." I smiled. "I haven't seen many chess champions."

"I read one yesterday," a colleague inserted.

"Well, we do have room for more than one chess champion. And

---

* In *Legally Blonde* and seemingly every other movie, the admissions committee is composed of a group of old, straight, white men outfitted with eyeglasses, tweed blazers, and bow ties. Hollywood couldn't have had it more wrong.

there's more to him than chess," the committee chair announced as he read the applicant's summary card projected on the wall. "He's ranked sixth in class and has impressive talent in languages."

"Which languages?" another colleague asked.

"Spanish and Italian."

"As does everyone else in this pool," the skeptical colleague responded. "Adios and ciao," he joked.

I cracked a smile. As harsh as my colleague was, he had a point. Many applicants spoke multiple languages. (And as a unilingual English speaker, I appreciated this type of talent. When I was growing up, the only other language spoken in my house was my mother's "Jersey City.")

"Well, let's slow down," the chair insisted. "What's he doing with his language talent?"

"It's hard to say," a colleague responded. "Nobody really speaks to it."

"Well, is there anything else the committee would like to discuss before voting?"

"His verbal score is on the low side for our pool," one colleague added.

"But his math score is nearly perfect," another announced.

The crowd sat silent for a while, pondering the master card. After a few moments, the chair called for a vote. "Admits?"

I raised my hand. (A chess champion who spoke three languages seemed impossibly impressive.)

"Defer?"

No hands raised. I sheepishly felt silly about my admit vote if none of the others in the room would even vote for a defer.

"Deny?"

Four hands raised.

"Another vote of 1–0–4. He's a deny. Moving on."

I was struggling. We were reading applications from tremendously interesting and engaged students, but we only had enough beds on campus for 10 percent of the pool. The rules had been simple. Deny most. Wait-list some. Admit few. But for each one we admitted, there were nine more who seemed just as good. It was *The Hunger Games,* college edition. Choosing one over another seemed impossible, if not ridiculous.

"Kate from Georgia is our next candidate," the committee chair announced. "She's a white female double legacy who placed twenty-first in a national competition for students interested in Greek literature."

"What did the readers say?" a colleague asked.

"She'd add to the class in that she wants to major in classics. And her essay about being a left-hander and advocating for more left-handed school supplies was well done."

"I'm convinced," a colleague commented. "We could use another classics major, and the double legacy is a bonus."

"I don't know," another colleague piped in. "Her recommenders say she's stronger in the sciences. Her lowest grade on her transcript is in Latin, and her Latin teacher's recommendation doesn't say much."

I studied the master card on the wall. It would be hard to deny Kate. She was ranked ninth in her class, had decent testing, and was involved in many activities. She was checking every box.

"Let's vote," the chair announced. "Admits?"

Two hands raised. Mine followed slowly.

"You're an admit, Becky?" the chair committee asked.

"I guess."

"Don't guess. Vote."

I contemplated my decision for a moment. Kate was amazing, certainly, but I didn't find her as appealing as others I had voted to admit. Perhaps it was time to be a bit more discerning. "Then, I'm a defer."

"So am I," another colleague said.

"As am I," the committee chair announced. "The vote is 2–3–0. She's a defer."

"Her parents won't be happy," a colleague who voted to admit muttered.

I took a deep breath. My change of vote determined this (nearly) perfect young person's future. *My* vote.

"Let's take a ten-minute break," the chair announced. "We're going to be here awhile."

I had decided to enter the admissions profession because I wanted to help people. I wanted to help them find their dream college. I wanted to help them navigate a difficult admissions process. I wanted to admit them.

I was now in the business of denying. I knew that a career at Dartmouth would mean rejecting a lot of applications. I wasn't naïve about the caliber of intellect required to keep up with the pace of Dartmouth's curriculum; however, seeing the strength of the pool made the rejections preposterous.

These kids were young Einsteins. And Winfreys. And Ginsburgs. They were going to change, save, and better the world. Each application brought something interesting to the table. Still, we could take only one in ten. The black belt or the prima ballerina? The teen *Jeopardy!* contestant or the newspaper cartoonist? The lead Sandy or the lead Danny? It was all too much.

"How's it going?" Tina, a more experienced colleague, asked me at the water cooler.

"Okay." I shrugged, not wanting to admit I was in over my head.

"I remember my first committee. I wanted to vote everybody in." She laughed at herself. "That was before I knew the secret to good admissions decisions."

My desperation for insight was likely leaking from my pores. "The secret?"

"Our decisions are about the whole of the college. Not about any one student."

"I don't understand." I shook my head.

"All of the students we've seen today are standouts nationally. But we need to select the standouts *in our pool.*"

"Okay," I said skeptically. "Then how do I recognize a standout in *our* pool?"

"Pay attention to the college profile. Find the students at the crossroads of the strongest tangible and intangible qualities. Those are the students who will make Dartmouth even more competitive."

"Do we need to be more competitive?"

She looked at me with a smirk. "*Every* college wants to be more competitive." She filled up her water bottle. "The more competitive pool we become, the more competitive pool we will attract. Remember, Becky, admissions isn't personal; it's business."

Business. The word left a sour taste in my mouth. I wasn't there for business. I was there for the people. I was there to change lives, grant opportunities, and recognize the next great talent.

But Tina had a point. While other colleagues publicly made the selection process sound magical, whimsical, and downright dreamy, Tina cut to the chase. We didn't have room for everyone. We didn't even have room for a quarter of the students in the pool. We didn't have room for all the Brazilian American students or all the field hockey goalies or all the history buffs or the chess champions.

Admissions officers were there to create a future class that would enhance the current campus community. At Dartmouth, and at many colleges across the country, admissions readers had to consider three priorities of the institution:

Increase diversity on campus. Our office valued diversity in the admissions process both to ensure opportunity for marginalized students and to enrich our community with individuals from various races, ethnicities, genders, and backgrounds. As officers, we reviewed all applicants in the context of their resources and social advantages. If given the opportunity, we'd act affirmatively to admit students who were not only talented in the classroom but also underrepresented on our campus. In our opinion, it was not only the right thing to do, but it was best for our college.

Maintain our selectivity. Strengthening our academic profile (and upping our standardized test average) was critical in proving our elitism in the rankings. It seemed the harder it was to get into a school, the more valued it was nationally. (Up until 2018, *U.S. News & World Report* used admissions data as a point of reference for its college rankings. Today, it considers "expert opinion" as a factor, likely leaning on folks' perception of the selectivity of these schools.)

Consider the needs of the college on a macro scale. We needed the smart (enough) child of the philanthropic billionaire for the development office.* We needed the football quarterback and the women's crew coxswain. (I'll speak more on athletic recruitment in chapter 16.) We needed VIP students with clout.† (Malala! Malia!) And we needed legacy‡ students to appease our alumni base. (Our policy during my time at Dartmouth was to give legacy applicants an extra review in the process. I strongly suggest that students with legacy ties clearly document these connections in the "family information" section or anywhere the question is asked.)

After every applicant was reviewed, we'd have the chance to tinker with the class to ensure our goals were met. If our profile was low

---

* If a student believes his family's wealth and philanthropic tendencies might be of interest, he should contact the development office directly. Development works directly with our dean to signal applicants of interest. (Word to the wealthy: even the wealthiest sometimes aren't wealthy enough.)

† We'd offer confidential, private tours for the children of celebrities, politicians, and folks of influence. One Hollywood A-lister declined a private tour offer, choosing to attend a regular crowded Saturday tour with his family. I'd always admired him on the screen, but his humility in being one of the many turned me into a superfan.

‡ At Dartmouth, legacy applicants were admitted at a greater rate than other applicants (nearly two and a half times the regular rate of admissions in 2011). While we weren't looking for a magical number of legacy admits, we would take legacy connections into consideration as a factor of many. Legacy preference continues to be a controversial admissions practice across American campuses.

on parochial students, we'd re-review applicants from the Academy of St. Someone. If we needed first-generation students, then those without college-educated parents might become swapped for those whose parents had multiple degrees. If our profile included students from all states except North Dakota, we'd re-review applicants in that demographic with pending wait list status. (Although we never felt like we needed students from every state, so if the North Dakotans weren't particularly strong that year, we wouldn't feel compelled to force the issue.)

But a robot could have done this work if the college only cared about an applicant's tangible qualities. An applicant's story also mattered in the business of admissions review. Intangible qualities described by teachers mattered. A student's perspective, energy, individuality, and narrative mattered. We weren't going to admit a student with amazing SAT scores unless she'd contribute something substantial besides verbal and math talents to the class. We weren't going to admit the next Gandhi unless his academic transcript matched his selflessness. And frankly, with so many students already qualified to be waiting at the admissions gate, the small details were the difference between students with similar SAT scores. (No computer formula would be able to decide among valedictorians.)

Of course, it was clear which SAT scores were strong for our pool. But the intangibles were blurrier. Only with more experience could I recognize which student narratives were more compelling additions to the Dartmouth class. The truth is that *experienced* diverse readers usually agreed on admissions outcomes. No matter what a reader's background, if he had seen enough of the pool and if he understood the current profile of the Dartmouth community, he would understand which applications raised the bar.

The more I read, the better reader I became. I began to recognize that creating a campus community is complex. (One difficult decision to admit a young man with VIP connections but questionable integrity still haunts me to this day.) I learned the depth of the waters. I knew which fish we threw back in the pool and which fish we kept. And like a salty old sea captain, I began to understand the seas on which our boat rocked.

"Here we have Peter, an Asian American male student ranked third in his class from Connecticut whose soccer team has won two state championships. He wrote an equally intellectual and entertaining essay on his collection of drought-tolerant plants and their place in the environment. His counselor calls him the 'true model of a gentleman scholar' and writes of his respect from faculty who don't have him in class."

It was our third and final day of early decision committee, and I was finally finding confidence in my admissions vote. As I read Peter's summary card, I recognized that his academic credentials were stronger than most in our pool. He was a contender in terms of raw SAT scores, AP scores, and GPA. Of course, we were looking for more.

"His English teacher calls him the best writer in the class," a colleague said as she read from the card projected on the wall. "Specifically, she says his nature writing is deserving of publication in science journals, even as a high schooler."

"His peer recommendation speaks of his unnatural ability to rally his peers to care about invasive plants," another colleague commented. "She says he inspired friends' curiosity about dangerous invasive hydrilla plants during spring break in Florida."

"What's hydrilla?" a colleague asked.

"Why don't you take some time to google it after we finish our vote," the chair said with a smile.

I leaned in a bit as my colleagues kept talking about Peter.

"He impressed his interviewer with his ability to talk articulately about ways to curb the town's opioid addiction problem," one read from the master card. "He's lent his talents to the town's official promotional campaign against prescription drug use and worked hard to change peers' minds even when deemed an uncool stance."

"And he wants to try college improv because his school has nothing like it," another chimed in. "Apparently, while he visited Dartmouth, he sat in on an improv practice because of his interest. He noted that even if he wasn't strong enough to make the group, he'd be excited to challenge the players with his scenario recommendations from the audience."

We had just read seven applications from bright, involved students from all over the country. But there was an energy about Peter's application that was different than the others. He was an intended English major who had already used his writing talent for other causes. (Dartmouth's humanities department would be strengthened by his interest in scientific writing.) He had a sense of humility about him. (Not everyone was going to make Dartmouth Improv, but having a passionate audience member would only strengthen their talents.) And his application was one of the strongest I'd seen in our pool in terms of tangible and intangible qualities. (His course load was noted as the strongest in his school by his counselor. She also noted that he wrote the "most relevant op-eds in the school newspaper's history.")

I might not have recognized it on the first day of committee, but as I sat there on the third day, I recognized a standout in the pool. Peter would specifically strengthen Dartmouth's community with his interdisciplinary writing talent. His SAT scores would strengthen the college's average. And he'd add to the student body as someone unafraid of peer pressure.

"Are we ready to vote?" the chair asked.

Heads nodded.

"Admits?"

I raised my hand confidently. Looking around the room, I realized everyone else did as well.

"Well, that was easy." The chair laughed as he recorded the vote.

It was the overstatement of the year. Making an admissions decision was never easy. Unless a school had a hundred percent admission rate, selecting a class was always going to have its challenges.

But on that rainy mid-December day as I sat at the early decision committee table, the job was becoming easier. My role in the process was becoming clearer. I was gaining perspective on the breadth and depth of the pool. I was recognizing that making decisions was about looking for the strongest students in the cross section of the quantitative and qualitative. I was understanding the importance of reflecting on the current Dartmouth class and working to strengthen that community. But most of all, I was gaining confidence in my vote.

Now, I'm regularly approached by people asking me how competitive college decisions are made. I tell them about the challenge of being a new reader and the ease of being more experienced. (I use the example that a person who reads one application will not have a sense of admissions' probability unless they read ten applications.) I urge them to recognize that all institutions make decisions based on their own pools and their own communities. I encourage them to complete thoughtful applications and apply to a range of schools. And I assure them that there are plenty of wonderful (and reasonably priced) institutions where our young people can thrive.

But what I emphasize the most is that college admissions is a business at nearly every institution. There can be (and are) tens of thousands of students standing at any one college gate. But in creating a class, admissions officers make decisions based on the overall strengths, needs, and statistics of *their own existing applicant pool.* There are pressures to strengthen the quantitative data of the class. There's a tension to add to the community that already exists on a campus. There's concern to select applicants whose tangible and intangible attributes would best enhance the college's own reputation, stature, and profile. A competitive college selection process is based on what's best for the college. Not what's best for the applicant.

What is best for the applicant is to be valued for her potential rather than the ranking of the college she attends. To learn for the sake of learning, to develop meaningful teacher relationships to prepare her for college professor relationships, and to be decent and kind to equally stressed-out peers. To take more pride on the path to the gate than on the name on the gate that swings open. And to be proud of the application put forward, regardless of the decisions she receives.

Admissions may be a business. But there are lots of businesses competing for students of many talents. There are multiple, glorious pools in which a fish can swim. There are other enticing hooks dangling in the water. And there are many hungry fishermen ready to make their catch.

THE COLLEGE SEARCH

CHAPTER TWO

FIRST STEPS

Learning the language of college is a lot like learning about the birds and the bees. Students become interested in the subject matter (especially when the older heartthrob from English class gets crushed by his first-choice institution). They seek information from reputable and not-so-reputable sources. (Some unfortunate kids absorb their information from back-of-the-bus Betsy.) And the more they learn, the more interested they become.

I met a lot of families who asked me when to start the college process. They wanted to know when they should buy test prep books, when to tour campuses, when to sit down with a counselor. For some, discussing the topic with their children was as daunting and anxiety producing as "the birds and the bees" conversation. With ridiculously competitive admissions rates, it seemed gaining an advantage in the college process meant starting early. But how early was too early?

Junior year is typically regarded as the official beginning of the application process. It's the time when folks start considering the application. The Common Application, which is a single application accepted by hundreds of American colleges, will be the application I primarily refer to in this book. (Hundreds of other colleges and universities in the United States have their own application preferences. For example, Georgetown, famously, does not accept the Common Application.) I warned families that they'd want to be taking action steps (test prep, college mailing sign-ups, researching colleges) by the middle of junior year to avoid being hit by the admissions tidal wave, which hits hard in the fall of senior year.

But before one strategizes testing, before one considers if he would be able to "go Ivy" (a term I've heard more times than I can count), before

one obsesses over community service hours, a student needs to consider
why (or why not) he should go to college. A student needs to learn the
basics of what college is, what it offers, and the many degrees available. A
student needs to recognize the difference between a college and a university, consider the meaning of financial aid "net price," and comprehend
the definition of a "liberal arts" curriculum. A student needs to take
baby steps.

I understand the obsession with a good start on the path to an "elite"
college. Alumni networks at competitive schools have long histories of
providing business opportunities through powerful (and loyal) hiring
networks. Parents want their students to be challenged academically
and given extensive resources to enhance their experiences. And many of
these institutions have the deep pockets to provide competitive financial
aid packages (when net price is considered).

Further, researchers continue to publish studies on the salary dis-
crepancies and job opportunities for those with diplomas from "top"
schools. In 2015, after factoring data from the U.S. Department of Education, Christopher Ingraham of the *Washington Post* concluded, "Ten
years after college graduation, the typical Ivy League graduate earns
more than twice as much as the typical graduate of other colleges." In
2015, a study led by Eric Eide, a Brigham Young University economics
professor, found that in the case of STEM-related majors, average earnings don't vary much between selective and less selective institutions.
In an alternative 2017 study by economists Raj Chetty, John Friedman,
Emmanuel Saez, Nicholas Turner, and Danny Yagan, lower-income students at top-ranked private schools appeared to have a better opportunity of reaching the top 1 percent of the earnings distribution than peers
at public universities. And a highly referenced 2018 study by researchers
Suqin Ge, Elliott Isaac, and Amalia R. Miller (which reexamined the
benchmark 1999 Dale and Krueger study) found no relationship between
college selectivity and long-term earnings for men, but women in this
same study had a different outcome depending on their marriage status,
with increased earnings for unmarried women. Academics continue to

examine the correlation of an "elite" college diploma with so-called success as recruiting markets change, technology advances, and the makeup of campus communities evolves and diversifies.

But there are many colleges to discover and many conversations to have before setting one's sights on a particular set of colleges. I believe the race to college should be more of a thoughtful stroll. It should begin with broad, informal conversation.

I'm not suggesting parents sit their children down, awkwardly announce that it's time for "the conversation," and start babbling on about need-based financial aid awards. I'm also aware that parents without college degrees will likely learn *alongside* their children as they navigate the college admissions process together. But college is a topic of conversation that regularly presents itself for discussion. During a March Madness game, a father can explain the merits of his technical school diploma while he cheers on Texas Tech. When Grandma announces that she's leaving her inheritance to historically Black colleges and universities, her grandkids can do research on the institutions before huffing about money. And when a mother overhears someone arguing that Princeton "is where the smart kids go," she can offer a more open-minded rebuttal. ("There are really smart kids on *every* campus, honey.")

Talking about college is appropriate at any age. But talking about *getting into* college sends a whole other message.

"It's time to start thinking about college," I announced to a room full of high school freshmen.

These words can send students into a panic because they infer:

It's time to start worrying about grades.
It's time to join the robotics team.
It's time to register for SAT prep classes.

I had volunteered to present to this group of freshmen from a nearby private New England high school even though I typically spoke only to upperclassmen. They had traveled to Dartmouth's campus by bus to take a tour and hear me speak. Although racially and physically diverse, they were a similar-looking group (as I found most first-year students to be). Perhaps they looked the same since they hadn't had much time to develop their own personal styles. Perhaps because half of them were wearing some sort of school-related sweat gear. Or perhaps it was because most students were lifelessly staring out the window.

I was tasked with inspiring them to start thinking about the college process, and the only reason I had agreed to present was because their counselor was a friend of mine. Ramona worked at a New England private school with expensive tuition and lousy teacher salaries. ("They spend more money cleaning the pool than they do on our benefits," she'd utter over cheap wine.) It was clear the parents expected a lot from her, even as a counselor of first-year students. For years, she had been asking me to speak with the freshmen about the college process "just to scare them into caring." And for years, I came up with excuses. I didn't enjoy speaking to underclassmen because my college-planning tips were limited for that audience. But after she dog-sat for me over Labor Day weekend, I owed her.

"Let's start with my top tips for college preparation."

The night prior, while simultaneously watching *Law and Order: SVU* reruns, I jotted down some presentation notes on a paper napkin. I'd given "College 101" presentations dozens of times to juniors and seniors, so I figured I'd just tweak my thoughts toward a younger audience. I had three helpful underclassmen tips.

1. **Take "challenging, yet appropriate" classes.**
We used the term "challenging, yet appropriate" often in college admissions to describe what type of curriculum we'd like to see on a transcript. These were classes that actively engaged the student who was prepared for the course material. There was no sense floating by with an easy A in regular biology if a more challenging honors option was available. There was no sense drowning in geometry honors if a regular-level geometry class would provide more time for homework.

We recognized that a student's high school ranking took nearly four years of high school into consideration. We understood that a student who would graduate valedictorian likely needed to have an incredible ninth grade. But junior and first-term senior grades mattered much more to admissions committees than first-year grades. I never voted to deny an applicant because of a freshman-year grade. (In fact, many admissions officers often speak of "upward trends" as strengths on applicants' transcripts.) And freshman (and sophomore) year were about trying new electives, dipping one's toes into curriculum that might not have been available in middle school, and challenging oneself to grow academically. In his first year, a high school student had some flexibility with his curriculum, providing he was forming a foundation for the years that followed.

Of course, it was still important to review overall school curriculum requirements so there would be no surprises by senior year. Which brought me to . . .

2. Familiarize oneself with the counseling office.

The counseling office is an underutilized resource, even before college application season. While many schools assign different counselors to students from year to year, a first-year counselor can still be helpful, even if she won't be the person who eventually writes one's college counseling recommendation. Underclassmen need to understand the big picture of high school: the curriculum tracks offered, higher-level classes that would require underclass prerequisites (i.e., you can't take anatomy in your junior year unless you take honors bio sophomore year), the various resources available. (Some students will take the PSAT as early as their sophomore year, and those borrowable PSAT test books on the guidance reference shelves aren't going to carry themselves out of the office.)

3. Develop writing skills.

My writing suggestion was by far my favorite tip, for both personal and professional reasons. Personally, I loved encouraging students to find their words. Professionally, I found that students who were strong writers wrote strong applications. Focusing on writing as an underclassman would help not only with the long college game but also with high school. I encouraged students to sharpen their skills through letter writing: op-eds to the school newspaper (about replacing the Coke machines with their other soft drink preferences), thank-you notes to teachers (who "forgot" to issue the detention for the uncovered book), love letters (signed, anonymous, or unsent) to a crush. The stronger one's writing, the easier one's application would be to complete.

These were helpful nuggets for underclassmen starting out on a college path. This was useful information that I wished I had received as a freshman. (Perhaps I would have introduced myself to my high school counselor earlier than junior spring.) But ten minutes into my talk, half the audience was looking out the window. The other half were fidgeting with whatever they wore on their wrists. Even Ramona had left the room. (I knew that she was likely somewhere on her phone flipping through online dating profiles away from the eyes of judgmental students.)

I'd lost them. These students couldn't become excited about choosing college prep coursework if they weren't excited about college. I'd have to rethink my attack. I decided to stop talking and start asking questions. (I thankfully remembered this good advice that I'd received from a public speaking workshop.) * "Why do you think someone would want to go to college?" I asked the young man wearing a SpongeBob SquarePants watch in the front row.

"Huh?" he asked, sitting up.

"Why do you think someone would want to go to college?"

"Because it would be cool to play on a college basketball team."

---

* One year, all admissions officers were required to attend a public speaking workshop hosted by the business school on campus. (We clearly weren't receiving positive feedback from visiting families on our oratory skills.) The one-day workshop didn't change the habits of the mumblers, the fast-talkers (like me), or the man who literally said "literally" twelve times per monologue. But it did teach us how to identify a bored audience.

"Are you a basketball player?"

"Yep." SpongeBob Watch nodded. "I'm the starting center. I want to play at UNC someday."

"Why UNC?"

"It has a good team and it's a good school."

"What makes it a good school?"

He breathed heavily in annoyance at my questioning. "I dunno. People say it's hard to get into."

I looked at SpongeBob Watch's classmates. "What other schools are hard to get into?"

Frank, back from the bathroom, called out without raising his hand. "The Ivies."

I turned to him. "Can you name the Ivies?"

"Well, Harvard and Yale, obviously." He paused. "Then, Brown, MIT, and Princeton."

"And Dartmouth," someone else offered. "That's why we're here listening to you."

"Don't forget Stanford," someone else announced. "It's basically just a group of the hardest schools to get into in the U.S."

"Stanford's not an Ivy," a young woman in a yellow cardigan spoke up. "Neither is MIT. What constitutes an Ivy has nothing to do with its competitiveness of getting in. Instead, the Ivy League was formed simply as an athletic conference."

A student sitting next to Yellow Cardigan rolled her eyes. As our conversation continued, it was clear that Yellow Cardigan knew a lot more about colleges and college admissions practices than her peers. When one classmate complained that she'd probably end up at a dumb state school like UVA, Yellow Cardigan mentioned that it's one of the hardest state schools to get into. When one classmate announced that he was going to "totally die of nerves" during his Harvard on-campus interview, she quietly explained that Harvard doesn't offer on-campus interviews. When a classmate said that everybody had to take the SATs, she whispered that there are SAT-optional schools.

Yellow Cardigan could have given my presentation. After she spoke about the differences between early decision and early action, I couldn't help but be in awe. "Where'd you learn so much about colleges?" I asked.

"My older sister." She shrugged. "We toured sixteen schools as a family last year. Columbia was by far the best. That's where I'm going to go."

There it was. There was no turning back for Yellow Cardigan. She knew what she wanted. She was officially a player.

"I'd never move to South America just to go to college," one of her classmates muttered before returning to pick at her nails.

In college admissions, we don't talk often to underclassmen. We don't want to be accused of perpetuating the frenzy. (Although we'll happily mail a fourth grader a brochure if he's interested.) Plus, we have little time for them as we obsess over the juniors and seniors.

But somewhere along the line, underclassmen become interested. It's not an overnight sensation but rather a gradual slide. (Typically, this doesn't happen with just my opening announcement that "it's time to start thinking about colleges.") Some take an early interest. Some come to the process later. But for many parents, it seems getting their children interested in college can't come fast enough.

"I know it's too early to be talking about this kind of stuff," my friend Uma said to me over lunch, "but I'm worried about Max's college résumé."

I had met Uma for portobello mushroom wraps, iced tea, and town gossip. I was off duty and uninterested in admissions talk (particularly because the last time I saw her son, he was still playing Little League). "Doesn't Max have one more year of middle school?"

"Nope." She took a sip of tea. "He's a freshman." She leaned across the table. "Although he's taller than Harry now. You should see him. He looks like he walked right off an NBA court."

"Does he play basketball?"

"No, no. I can't get him interested."

"Is he still playing baseball?"

"No, he never really loved team sports." She bit a chickpea from her fork, then leaned forward. "To be honest, he's not interested in much. I'm worried about his college résumé. Nothing seems to excite him."

Of course, things excited him. But beating his friends at fast-food milkshake chugging contests wasn't quite what she had in mind. "Doesn't he have a thing for comic books? Wasn't Harry searching for some rare comic book for him for Christmas last year?"

Uma nodded. "He loves comic books. But that's not going to build his résumé." She put down her fork. "He's been considering band. But I'm not sure he'll stick with it. But won't that look bad if he only plays the trumpet for a year?"

"Not any worse than if he never played the trumpet."

"I know I sound like one of those crazy parents." * She laughed. "But I just want to help best prepare him for college."

I pictured my friend dragging her son to band practice while he ninja-gripped his comics and milkshakes. "You do sound like a crazy parent." I laughed, too. "He'll be fine."

"I know, I know." She nodded. "But Becky," she leaned in and whispered, "will he be?"

I had known Uma for years. She was a warm, caring mother who wanted the best for her children. But her concern about college preparedness was premature. She instead should have been concerned about her son's *high school* preparedness. If he had few interests besides milkshakes and comic books, he was losing the opportunity to experiment with the many opportunities high school provides.

Underclassmen should practice good habits in high school for the

---

* If I had a dollar for every time this was muttered to me, I'd be a thousandaire.

sake of *high school.** They should learn for the sake of learning. They should pick up a paintbrush, an oar, or a trumpet because it's a great time to experiment. And they should engage in something, anything, to become curious citizens of the world. All these things will help them as college applicants. But more importantly, it will help them as *people.*

If freshmen want to "best prepare" themselves for college, they can introduce themselves to their school counselors and work on their writing. They can work hard in challenging classes that will serve as the framework for the rest of their high school career. They can perfect the chemistry of a well-blended strawberry and Oreo milkshake, if milkshakes are their thing. But there was no sense obsessing about college when they should have been obsessing about high school.

Of course, as they did with the birds and the bees, students will come to this process on their own terms. There will always be one peer among the group who seems to know it all, seemingly "advanced" in her knowledge. In this case, Yellow Cardigan was thinking about the goal line, she knew what she wanted, and she was paving the path to Columbia. Uma's son, Max, on the other hand, was a late bloomer. He didn't seem interested in the college process yet, let alone the high school experience.

But was Yellow Cardigan going to be admitted to a more competitive school because she learned the language of college earlier?

Was Max going to blow his chances of college admission by having a blank résumé for the entirety of his ninth-grade year?

It was too early to tell.

In my years of working in admissions, it was clear that a lot could change in four years. Yellow Cardigan could burn out (or realize that the local state school was her best option). Max could have an extracurricular breakthrough. (He could be the finest illustrator in Marvel's future.) I

---

* As an admissions director, it pained me when parents spoke of college admission as a prize or punishment. Students were under enough pressure. One father described "getting into an Ivy" as "the prize for straight As." I dry heaved as the words escaped his mouth. Getting into college shouldn't be a prize. The education itself is the prize.

couldn't tell a darn thing about an applicant's chances of being admitted to Dartmouth by solely looking at his first-year academic and extracurricular record. But I could tell if a first-year student was setting himself up to thrive in his sophomore year. And that's all that really mattered.

There's already enough pressure on our young people. Rates of teenage anxiety have reportedly mounted in recent years for a myriad of reasons.* Underclassmen will become interested in the route to college on their own timelines. But we can start general conversations about college (and not the process) early. We can nip preconceptions in the bud. We can discuss what the fuss is about by reminding ourselves what the fuss is about. ("Son, college is an opportunity for people to learn more from their professors, from their peers, from their resources. It's not just about going Ivy.") We can do our best to preserve high school as an important experience on its own.

After forty minutes, my time with the freshmen was over. I'd let them talk for twenty minutes. I'd talked for twenty minutes. I was incredibly interested in what they had to say. They seemed less so in what I had to say. But we'd all survived the presentation.

I needed to make a final point before letting them go. I'd bore them with a monologue. I'd scare them with a heavy hand. But there was room for one last nudge. "The most important thing you can do to prepare for college is to go to high school."

"Well, that's obvious," the girl in the front muttered.

"Maybe so," I said. "But it's the most critical step. High school is the building block to what's next."

---

* Reports from the Centers for Disease Control note that depression and anxiety have increased in our children. In a 2016 Higher Education Research survey, nearly 41 percent of incoming college freshman students said they felt "overwhelmed by all they have to do." In 2001, 28 percent of students responded "yes" to the same question, while in 1985 the number was only 18 percent.

"People go to high school without going to college."

"They do. But nobody goes to college without going to high school. *
What a student takes out of high school is what she will bring to college.
The more she makes of high school, the more interested a college will be
in her offerings."

It was my most heartfelt comment of the day. And to my surprise,
some (but certainly not all) seemed moved by my words.

Ramona, who had returned to the classroom, smiled while looking at
her watch. "Now, we just have time for one question before we let Mrs.
Sabky go back to her important work. Let's make it a good one."

Two hands raised from the group. Unsurprisingly, one hand belonged
to Yellow Cardigan. Knowing that her question was about AP tests,
music supplements, or some other sophisticated topic, I decided to call
on the other person. I was excited that I had made an impact on more
than one member of the audience and I was curious to hear what she had
to say.

The young woman in the navy sweatshirt tilted her head to the side
as she spoke. "Is there a place around here to buy decent iced coffee
before we board the bus?"

A smirk rose on my face. College could wait. But obviously being a
freshman could not.

---

* Although many colleges (like Dartmouth) don't require high school diplomas, I'd
  never heard of a student who went to college without completing the majority of
  high school.

CHAPTER THREE

CREATING THE RIGHT COLLEGE LIST

There are more than five thousand colleges and universities in the United States. The popular *Fiske Guide to Colleges* features about three hundred of these institutions. Many of these schools will mail brochures to anyone who registered for the SAT. (All of these brochures feature professors at blackboards, students at microscopes, and impossibly gleeful frisbee players on autumnal quads.) A college-bound student will (likely) attend one of these schools. But before he tours campuses, submits applications, and sits in on classes, he needs to create a college list. In order to create the *right* college list, he needs to do his homework.

"I'm applying to Brown, Tufts, and Dartmouth," Marco, a rising senior and a family acquaintance, shared with me at a summer picnic.

"That's a competitive group," I said. "Are you applying anywhere else?"

"Well, I mean I'll apply to State X and State Y as well," he said as an afterthought. "But only because my counselor basically encourages everyone in our school to apply there."

"I love State X and State Y." I smiled.

"They're good schools." He shrugged. "But they're not Brown or anything."

"Have you visited Brown?"

"I'm going next weekend. But it's been at the top of my list forever."

I've never helped a student come up with a college list. (I strongly encourage that students lean on their counselors, trusted teachers, and vetted college guides to develop their lists of schools of interest.) My job was solely to encourage people to apply to Dartmouth.

But I have observed many families going through the process. I have witnessed their mistakes and their triumphs. And I have met students who seemed to be applying to schools for all the wrong reasons (i.e., the Singapore student who wanted to go to Dartmouth because she loved Meredith Grey, the fictional character and Dartmouth alumna from the popular television show *Grey's Anatomy*).

I didn't know if Marco would be admitted to Brown. I knew little about his interests, record, or hobbies. But I did know that Brown was a tough nut to crack. I knew that making a preferred college list of three schools with incredibly competitive admissions rates was bad news. And I knew that applying to schools he wasn't excited about attending was even worse.

People ask me how many schools to add to their college lists. I don't have a definitive answer. My best response is as many schools as one can comfortably visit either before (or after) application season. (I recognize that not everyone can visit every college, but I'll speak more on this topic in the next chapter.) Applying to twenty schools seems outlandish (and expensive without fee waivers). Applying to all eight Ivies seems pretentious (as some of the schools really have little in common with each other besides the Ivy stamp). Applying to only two schools seems too much of a gamble. What seemed to matter more than the number of schools is the range of competitiveness, match, and genuine interest.

Of course, as an application reviewer, a candidate's college list was irrelevant. I didn't seek out this information while reading applications. In person, though, I sometimes asked a student about his college list out of curiosity. Many Dartmouth applicants applied to similar overlap schools: Middlebury, Amherst, Duke, and Tufts. Some Dartmouth applicants surprised me with their lists. (I loved hearing from students applying to both liberal arts schools and music conservatories.) And every so often, a student inspired me to research a school of which I'd never heard.

Developing a college list was clearly intimidating to some students. But after witnessing so many families struggle with this process, it was clear to me that there are actionable steps a student can take to ensure her list is both practical and inspiring.

1. Get excited about more than one school.

Applying to college isn't marriage. A student can fall in love (or at least like) with multiple schools. It's natural to have a front-runner. (And I'm a firm believer in applying early decision. I'll speak about this more in chapter 14.) But it's also dangerous to believe that only one institution could be a happy fit.

2. Use a college's average standardized testing data and its admissions rate as an admissions probability guide.

Testing is a thorn in everybody's side. But it does provide useful data in determining the competitiveness of one's college list. As colleges receive more applications, admissions outcomes will become more unpredictable. Using tangible college data points can help a student build a list with a range of selectivity and average standardized scores.

3. Become realistic about finances and college affordability.

Any time is a good time to have a conversation with family and counselors—both school and financial—about college payment potential. ALL schools on one's list should be personally affordable (with little student debt), even without outside scholarships. Many colleges and universities offer net price calculators online to allow families to estimate their out-of-pocket costs.

4. Apply only to colleges one wants to attend.

I've never liked the term "safety school." Nobody bubbles over with excitement about a safety choice. ("I ended up at my safety school" is a very different statement than "I was admitted to the University of X.") But just because a school has less competitive admission rates doesn't mean it's less fabulous. Wonderful schools of all competitive admissions rates are out there and waiting. And NO college (especially at the cost of some tuitions) should ever feel like a consolation prize.

A few months later, I ran into Marco at the grocery store. "I'm going to State Y," he told me as we chitchatted over the red pepper bin.

"That's terrific! Are you excited?"

"My best friend is going there," he replied (not answering my question). "So there's that."

In the next few minutes, I would come to find out that State Y was Marco's best friend's "reach school." Marco was denied by the other schools to which he applied. He believed it was crazy that he, in the top 10 percent of his class, and his best friend, in the top 40 percent, were ending up at the same institution.

It was crazier to me that his family was planning on spending sixty grand a year for out-of-state tuition for a school he was shrugging off. "I'm sure you'll like State Y," I said with a smile. I knew plenty of other students who attended and loved their experience.

"It'll be fine," he said as he poked at a pepper.

College is a privilege. State Y is a terrific institution. Marco's matriculation should have been more than just "fine." ("Fine" should be reserved for meal options at an airport, or blind date outcomes, or drinking Pepsi when a restaurant has run out of Coke.) It saddened me to hear Marco speak this way of his higher education path. I couldn't help but wonder if he was disappointed by his option because of his denials elsewhere. Or, perhaps, he simply hadn't kept an open enough mind when first considering schools. (I can assure students that having an open mind will lead to more open doors.)

I couldn't personally help students like Marco widen (or narrow) their lists. I couldn't assure them that they'd like Florida State over the University of Florida. I couldn't assist them in identifying New England universities with math majors and debate teams. (There are too many to count.) And I couldn't comment on what they'd personally like (or dislike) about any one campus.

But I could tell them to keep reading the brochure that caught their eye. I could tell them to visit the University of Notre Dame if (for no good reason) they've wanted to attend since they were youngsters. I could tell them to open their minds while listening to their guts. I could tell them to do their homework (on top of their *homework*).

I recognize that many students can't afford more than community college. I know that some students are limited in their college scope because of financial, physical, or familial circumstances. But I also know that *anyone* investing time and resources in postsecondary education cares about her future. And students who did their homework before they applied tended to be more pleased with their choices come spring.

Every college in America has the potential to change a student's life. I hope that those with the freedom to make choices can think critically about how and why they are making their decisions. I hope they care more about personal opportunity than rankings. (The two do not necessarily go hand in hand.) I hope they dare to consider schools outside the box. And, above all, I hope they are excited about what's to come.

CHAPTER FOUR

THE CAMPUS VISIT

Americans love our college tours. They're the subject of movies, country club conversations, and online blogs. In many ways, visiting a college is as touristy as it is practical, as whimsical as it is serious, as enjoyable as it is intimidating.

A visit to campus captures the spirit of the college in a way unlike any brochure or university marketing campaign can. (You can't smell the stench from the fraternity row dumpsters by reading a pamphlet.) Most colleges have impeccably landscaped quads, unlimited dining hall home fries, and interlibrary loan policies to make Barnes and Noble sweat. It's no surprise people travel thousands of miles to sample the goods.

I recognize not everyone can visit his colleges of choice. These folks can still do significant research from afar to gain a sense of a school before applying. They can take virtual tours, participate in admissions online chats, or browse the many web pages curated by the college. Regardless of whether a student intends on visiting a campus, I encourage ALL students to do the following before applying to a college.

- Read online campus newspapers (especially the op-eds that spill the beans of what matters to the student body and why).
- Reference the course catalogue (to understand the specific requirements for that forensics science major). *

---

* It's a fact that one of every four students at any given college fair I attended wanted to be the next CSI investigator.

- Contact the admissions office to see if they offer resources to students unable to make the trip. Some offices offer funding for admitted students to attend on-campus yield events. ("Yield" is admissions insider's lingo for events centered around admissions matriculation.) Some offices have student workers who are happy to Skype with prospective students. Other offices would happily put a prospective student in touch with a local alum.

But those with the time and the resources should make the trip. In planning their visit:

- Students should visit whenever classes are in session. (I'd specifically encourage a Friday afternoon visit, followed by a night spent on or near campus to experience the best and worst of a weekday AND a weekend.)
- They should ask about special community-related admissions programming. (At Dartmouth, we hosted an annual Indigenous Fly-In program for students interested in connecting with our Native community. *)
- They should preregister with the admissions office to receive demonstrated interest credit. (Many colleges use demonstrated interest to figure how seriously a candidate may be considering a school.[†] Registering for a campus tour was one way to demonstrate one's interest, but so was opening an e-mail from the office, or simply calling the regional officer and stating, "I'm interested.")

---

* A college "Fly-In" program was a subsidized visit to campus for students of defined backgrounds and/or low socioeconomic status. At Dartmouth, we typically hosted one or two of these programs annually.

[†] There are glaring problems with using demonstrated interest, of course. Less-resourced students don't have the same opportunities to prove their commitment. Tracking these interactions took technology and human resources. And it created a culture of obsession.

In my time at Dartmouth, I would estimate that tens of thousands of people visited our admissions office. They came with school trips and parents, coaches, and counselors. They carried umbrellas, bus tickets, and well-charged iPhones. Some fell in love immediately. Others "didn't like the feel." But all eyes widened with possibility as they walked up the front steps of the admissions building, McNutt Hall.

In my opinion, McNutt itself wasn't very impressive. During my tenure, it was home to the occasional bat and more often the rodent. There was little parking, little signage, and few welcome* details on the building. (In 2007, a Canadian artist constructed an Inuksuk on the front lawn, but unless a student stopped to read the dedication on the Inuit art, he probably wouldn't understand the significance.) The admissions lobby† was on the second floor, a significant stair climb from the building's heavy, wooden front doors. And the restroom doors swung inward, leaving little room to circumnavigate the toilet without touching the porcelain.

One might think that we didn't care about our visitors. (*Darling, prospective students should be honored to breathe in dust particles from Dartmouth's forefathers.*) But the truth was that we did care. We *wanted* visitors. We wanted their application fees. Like so many competitive universities, we wanted their applications for their overall numbers. The more applications we received, the lower our admissions rate. The lower our admissions rate, the more elite we appeared. (We just

---

* One year, a well-meaning and successful computer science project aimed at environmentalism was constructed at the base of the admissions stairs. It used a polar bear animation to showcase how well our building was conserving resources. Considering that our office didn't conserve resources well, the polar bear often would be walking on disappearing ice caps. It wasn't the best first impression for our visitors.

† The Dartmouth lobby was a far cry from most admissions lobbies. When I worked at St. Lawrence University, our lobby had oriental carpets, an inviting fireplace, and the occasional warm chocolate chip cookie at the front desk.

budgeted more money for invitations to campus than on admissions décor.) *

Thankfully, they came. They came in droves. And after they checked in with the receptionist and poured a cup of cheap coffee, it would be my turn to convince them Dartmouth was better than its lobby. I'd put on the razzle-dazzle for the masses.

"And if we don't have a major of your choosing, you can design your own," I said as I gallivanted across the floor like P. T. Barnum.

I'd given the on-campus information session hundreds of times and still loved the limelight. (I believe every admissions officer secretly wanted to be a cabaret star at some point in her life.) It was the same old thing to a new crowd of people. *Dartmouth could be everything to everyone.* I showed slides featuring students in front of equation-filled chalkboards and faculty in front of students sitting on the quad. (There was no mention of frat basements, frostbite, or concerns about faculty diversity.) I talked about the invention of BASIC[†] on campus, leaving out the invention of beer pong.

And after years of practice (and the occasional misfire), I knew what resonated. Heads nodded when I discussed the importance of a liberal arts curriculum. (*"Even the most steadfast scientist can find something relevant in Shakespeare."*) Mothers giggled when I instructed their children to choose the top bunk. (*"The bottom bunk turns into a communal couch."*) Alumni nodded as I waxed poetic about the homecoming days of yore. (*"Rah, rah, Dartmouth!"*)

---

* In later years, our office finally swapped out the old, dusty furniture for a more modern look.

† BASIC is a computer programming language, invented on Dartmouth's campus in 1964.

As I talked, they leaned in. It didn't matter that they'd heard the same thing from Tufts, Marist, and the University of Michigan. It didn't matter that the photograph of a student sitting in a chair reading a book could have been taken anywhere. It didn't matter that I had no idea what constituted a classics curriculum. All that mattered was that Dartmouth could be theirs. (For a price, of course. But had I mentioned the MAGICAL FINANCIAL AID PACKAGES?!)

I insisted that with a Dartmouth degree, students could become U.S. presidents, circus clowns, and cartoon animators. They could visit Antarctica or study primates in Madagascar. They could find community regardless of their ethnicity, political party, or Major League Baseball loyalty. (Even our Red Sox–loving community embraced tolerance toward Yankees fans.) There was nothing they couldn't be or do or see or become.

The purpose of my information session was to appeal to a wide audience. I was giving each student what he wanted. Dartmouth was both a college and a university. (While technically named a college for both historical reasons and its focus on undergraduate students, Dartmouth was home to many graduate schools, making it more of a university.) It was small and large (depending on one's perspective). It had the perks of a rural location yet a calendar that allowed folks to study abroad in cities far longer than our competitor colleges. It was everything anyone could want.

I was selling the dream. The students were my target consumers. And this, like every other college information session, was business.

Many college campuses look similar.* Many admissions officers sound the same. Many universities seem interchangeable. Most students would learn and thrive at many of these schools. This is a wonderful thing. This

---

* The library tower at Colby College, my alma mater, was an exact replica of the library tower at Dartmouth (which itself was modeled after Independence Hall in Philadelphia).

is a testament to the many institutions providing both the breadth and depth of curriculums to prepare our young people for the workplace, the community, the world stage.

But colleges are different. While admissions presents its best college overview, it's important that prospective students research their individual preferences. At this point of the application process, the student is in the position of power. He is choosing where to apply. (After the application, the college is in the position of power. Then, after admission, the student is powerful once again.) And while colleges will send students on tours (with articulate and adorable tour guides), there's more to campus than beautiful library towers.

"We flew here from Iowa." The student smiled at me after returning to the admissions lobby post-tour. "Des Moines, specifically."

"Wonderful," I responded. "How are you enjoying things?"

"So far, so good. We enjoyed both the information session and the tour."

"What else are you seeing while you're in town?"

"Well, I'm interested in premed and heard you have a new science center. We didn't see it on the tour, but I was hoping to swing by before I head back to Boston."

"Yes, the Class of 1978 Life Sciences building. It's on the far side of campus but definitely worth the walk."

The student paused before speaking. "How far?"

I shrugged. "Probably about a half mile."

He paused for a moment while he looked over his shoulder at his parents, who were sitting on a nearby couch, browsing a pamphlet. "It's a bit cold* out there today. Maybe I'll see it next time."

---

* It was late October. They had yet to understand the meaning of "cold" in New Hampshire. By January, we'd form frost on our nose hair during our coffee runs.

"Are you sure? There's a lot right next to the building if you just want to drive down there and park."

He shook his head. "Nah, it's all right. But if you could point me in the direction of the bookstore, that'd be great." He leaned in with a smile. "Can't head home without a sweatshirt!"

I wanted to lie and tell Mr. Des Moines that the campus bookstore was a thirty-minute walk. (It was five.) I wanted to tell him that sweatshirts were reserved for students who visited the academic buildings of their interest. I wanted to grab him by the hand and march him down to the science center.

But I didn't. "Down the street, through the light, and on the right," I said.

Most students weren't as lackadaisical as Mr. Des Moines. Most visitors to campus were happy to take a few extra steps to see the hockey rink, the economics department, or the ceramics studio. But in my opinion, stepping outside the typical parameters of a college visit was crucial to not only understanding a college better but writing a stronger application

On application supplements, most colleges ask a form of "Why Our College?" (Dartmouth's verbose* supplement wins points for its self-marketing.) Students who made the most of a campus visit often had better answers to this question. They were more specific, more authentic, more insightful. For example:

---

* A required 2019 supplemental question for Dartmouth read: *While arguing a Dartmouth-related case before the U.S. Supreme Court in 1818, Daniel Webster, Class of 1801, delivered this memorable line: "It is, Sir . . . a small college. And yet, there are those who love it!" As you seek admission to the Class of 2023, what aspects of the College's program, community or campus environment attract your interest?*

A budding computer scientist might speak about witnessing knot-tying robots at Dartmouth's Reality and Robotics Lab.

A student interested in LGBTQ issues might have a relevant comment on the college's commitment to gender-neutral bathrooms after meeting with students at Dartmouth's Triangle House.

A lover of baking might gush about the pastry quality on campus. (Pastries might not be the most important reason to choose a college, but I couldn't fault someone for admiring the sweetness of our raspberry jam bars.)

Granted, in order to have something specific to share, a student needed to experience more than the regularly scheduled admissions programming. For those who couldn't visit, a supplemental essay could still be specific if he researched (or engaged with) a department, club, or community on a deeper level. But if a student could visit, he must be his own campus investigator.

I found that sometimes students felt like they needed permission to wander off the beaten path. As long as students were abiding by school policies (i.e., no visitors in campus dorms for security reasons), most students were welcome in college public spaces. Most current college students loved chatting up prospective high school students, if approached. And faculty members seemed open to speaking with families (providing the visitors were respectful of their time).

I was delighted when I met a high school senior who had already visited the equestrian center and the French department before her tour. I was impressed when a student (kindly) asked our admissions student receptionist what *she* liked most about the school. I was taken with a young man who bothered to ask if it was permitted to swing by the college radio station.

But what mattered more than my opinion on these young people was their own initiative for leaving no stone unturned. When speaking to other students who wanted to make the most out of their visits, I encouraged them to:

EAT IN THE DINING HALL.

In my opinion, the dining hall is a "must see" on campus but not for reasons one would imagine. It's not about the pizza (although, it's *always* about the pizza) but rather the people. (Many colleges, including Dartmouth, would allow the public to dine for the price of a meal.) It's a place to witness campus energy. It's a place to notice who was sitting with whom. It's a place to eavesdrop* on what the student in the ski hat says to the student with the guitar case as they ladle chowder at the soup station. It's a place to hear conversations on campus that weren't scripted, biased, or peppered with overused phrases such as "intellectual curiosity."

CONTACT AN ADVISOR OF A STUDENT CLUB OR COMMUNITY AND ARRANGE A MEETING.

If time allowed, our campus rabbi would happily meet a prospective family for tea. Same for the international student advisor, the assistant softball coach, and the robotics professor. These folks' primary job was to assist current college students, but in my experience, they'd be happy to talk to a prospective family (provided they had the time).

Most college faculty and staff e-mail addresses can be found through department or club web pages. There is no harm in reaching out to folks affiliated with communities of interest, introducing oneself, mentioning an upcoming visit, and asking the best way to learn more about their

---

* I'm a strong advocate for eavesdropping in the dining hall. I also support eavesdropping on campus sidewalks, in line for the library bathroom, and while waiting for that uncomplicated-but-taking-too-long green smoothie in the campus café.

organization. Often, students were surprised by how willing our faculty and staff were to engage with passionate prospectives.

ROAM THE HALLWAY OF A PREFERRED ACADEMIC DEPARTMENT.

Tour guides will do their best to talk about the academic experience. But as someone who has shadowed umpteen college tours, it's clear that tour guide presentations are greatly contingent upon the tour guide's major. (Math majors have a lot to say about STEM, less to say about Spanish.) If a student is seriously interested in a department, he'd best go right to the source.

On many campuses, academic buildings remain open to the public during school hours. (Some colleges and universities have differing security policies, so check before visiting.) If possible, a prospective student should visit the academic department of her choosing, read the announcement board, notice if professors' doors are open, and decide if people seem happy. If a student has serious interest in a potential major, it's worth taking a few extra steps to survey the department's resources, energy, and environment. (At one unnamed college I visited as an undergraduate, the English department offered cozy, quiet reading spaces with a shelf of "Unrequired Reading" borrowable books. I was hooked.)

READ THE ANNOUNCEMENTS ON THE STUDENT CENTER BOARD.

Are people protesting plastic straws? Is Twitter recruiting interns on campus? Is Grace Potter playing in the student center? Is someone offering Segway lessons in exchange for macroeconomics tutoring? Where students are focusing their energy says a lot about the student experience. Paying attention to campus announcements (whether posted or online) can help a student understand a college's major priorities (i.e., Greek life, activism, internships, etc.).

College is an investment. Even at colleges with low admit rates, students are *consumers*. There is no use listening to an admissions officer talk about the engineering school on campus when a student could walk next door and experience it in person. A campus visit is a student's chance to see what he wants to see (and not just what the college wants to show him). This is a chance to turn over a few rocks, peek backstage, and take a test-drive of an institution. And while many prospective students will return to visit campus once admitted (and many students will only visit campus *after* being admitted), every opportunity to learn more should be maximized.

After I was done razzle-dazzling the audience at my information session, families lined up for face time. They asked questions about our study abroad programs, double majors, and testing policies. They pushed résumés (which I wouldn't collect), flashed smiles, and did their best to leave an impression.

One woman, wearing both a pearl necklace and a nose ring, extended her hand. I recognized her as the student who correctly answered my question about Dr. Seuss's real name* during the presentation. (There was one in every group who could answer the question and many in every group who wished they'd had the answer.) "I feel dumb for asking," she began, "but I heard that Dartmouth has its own orchid collection. Is this true?"

"It is. It's in the campus greenhouse."

"Is it open to the public?"

I nodded. "It will feel nice and balmy in there on a cold day like today."

---

* Theodor Geisel, aka Dr. Seuss, is a Dartmouth super alum. We used his characters and likeness ad nauseam.

"Do you think you could give me directions?"

"Sure. Do you grow orchids?"

"No." She laughed. "But I work part-time at a floral shop in the summers. Orchids have become my favorite flower. I find them interesting."

Interesting, I thought to myself. I'd been asked about a lot of places on campus, but I had never been asked about our orchid collection. "The greenhouse is down in the new Class of 1978 Life Sciences Center. It's a bit of a walk but certainly worthwhile."

"Great," she responded enthusiastically as she handed over a campus map. "I'd like to explore the far side of campus anyway. I did come all the way from Atlanta."

I pulled out a pen and circled the greenhouse. "I haven't even asked your name."

"Hannah. Hannah from Atlanta. Lover of orchids and all things Dr. Seuss."

Hannah and I spoke for a few more minutes. She told me about her interest in presidential history, her passion for American Sign Language, and her commitment to field hockey. I knew that by the time she applied to Dartmouth, I likely wouldn't remember much about these interests. I wouldn't remember her pearls and nose ring combination (which was intriguing), and I certainly wouldn't recall that she knew the answer to my Dr. Seuss question. (After dozens of information sessions annually, those who knew Theodor Geisel's name started to blur.)

I might not even remember that she was the young woman who asked for directions to the orchid collection. But I had a feeling that our greenhouse would be mentioned in her application. I had an inkling that she'd have more interesting things to say on her supplement than Mr. Des Moines. And I was sure that she'd leave campus with a better understanding of the college than those who had stuck to the script.

CHAPTER FIVE

COMING TO A HIGH SCHOOL NEAR YOU

If a student couldn't travel to campus, there was still a chance we'd meet in person. For approximately five weeks every fall and three weeks every spring, I and most other admissions officers would pack up breath mints, hand sanitizer, and business cards* and hit the road. We'd recruit, we'd schmooze, and we'd circle school parking lots for visitor spaces. It was a significant component to the job, and it was a lovely escape from campus.

A person can tell a lot about an admissions officer by his regional travel territory. The officer responsible for Manhattan is usually the officer without a driver's license. The officer responsible for Central Florida is usually the officer with a passion for all things Disney. The officer responsible for Hawaii is usually a seasoned expert who fought for her trip to the islands. And the officer with Ohio was usually the rookie. (As much as we all appreciated the Buckeye State, nobody was positioning for Dayton.)

For most of my career, I was the admissions representative for New Jersey and South Florida. (My other U.S. territories fluctuated between places like Colorado, Arkansas, Utah, Northern California, Long Island, Tennessee, Nevada, and Louisiana.) Other admissions officers groaned at the prospect of traveling the Garden State, but for me, as a New Jersey native, it was home. (Listening to Springsteen never felt as right as when "Rosalita" blasted in my rental car on the Jersey Turnpike.) South Florida

---

* Callers to our office suffered a long phone tree of options. Sometimes, by the time they got me on the phone, they'd already spoken to two other support staff members.

was basically a gift from the travel manager for taking New Jersey. A seafood-filled, sunshine-soaked gift.

It's important for a prospective student to know his regional officer. (Typically, colleges publish each admissions officer's responsibilities and travel plans online. If this information is not available, a student can usually call for this information.) It's important not because he can write a *Toy Story* essay to pull at the heartstrings of the Central Florida officer, but rather to form a relationship with the person who will best represent and review his candidacy. Knowing the territory manager is important because this person:

- Will likely be the first person to read, take notes on, summarize, and vote on one's application.
- Will present the application in committee, if necessary.
- Will be responsible for familiarizing herself with an applicant's school context.
- Will review the application if wait-listed.
- Will conduct recruitment travel to the area.

Students don't need to befriend admissions officers. But introducing themselves (in person or via e-mail) can be helpful if there are special circumstances down the line (e.g., the wait list).

Of course, just because I was visiting an applicant's state didn't mean I would necessarily be meeting the applicant. There was never enough time on the road to visit every high school of interest. (There are over five hundred high schools in New Jersey, and I'd have time to visit only about thirty-five.) The business of recruitment travel was dependent on drumming up more applications. I was pressed to visit large schools with strong numbers of college-bound graduates. I was encouraged to rev the pipelines at "feeder schools." And I wanted to partner with community-based organizations that identified talent in underserved communities. The politics of recruiting a diverse and talented class were at work while I crafted my itinerary.

Still, I was able to meet many, many students while on the road. (In addition to meeting students at school visits, I also met those who attended the regional public information sessions and area college fairs.) I estimate that I met one thousand students a year while recruiting off campus. Tall students. Short students. Quiet students. Chatty students. Nearly all these young people were bright and interesting. I enjoyed meeting them, walking their school hallways, and recruiting them to apply. I knew I wouldn't remember all of them. But occasionally, someone would catch my attention.

Mockingbird High was a diverse, large public school in suburban Florida. Like many others in its area, it had balmy hallways, limited visitor parking, and a football stadium larger than most. I'd been there for twenty minutes, presenting to a group of five students in a classroom, trying to professionally wipe sweat from my brow as I spoke.

Despite being the only woman in a group of five students, Layla didn't capture my attention immediately. She, like the others, had spent most of her time nodding appropriately while I babbled on. It wasn't until I opened the floor for questions that she showed her true colors.

"How long is your book-borrowing policy?" Layla asked.

"Our what?"

"Book borrowing. How long can a student keep a book out of the library at a time?"

I knew a lot about Dartmouth's library. I bragged a lot about its two million volumes, its Orozco art murals, and its Dr. Seuss room. But I had no idea how long a student could keep out a library book.

"I'm not sure. A few weeks, I think."

"That's better than our library. And how many books can I take out at a time?"

"Twelve, maybe? Or twenty? There might not be a limit. I don't know, but I can find out."

"You're not going to have time for reading in college," one of the young men scoffed.

"There's always time for reading," she corrected him before turning to me. "Don't worry about it. I was just curious."

Calling herself curious was an understatement. The young men asked me typical questions. (*What's the most popular major? Can students study abroad more than once? Are there freshman dorms?*) But Layla asked me questions others hadn't thought to ask. (*What percentage of professors are tenured? Can students receive daily newspaper deliveries? Are first-year students allowed to request non-native English-speaking roommates?*)

She stumped the heck out of me. And as frustrating as it was not to have answers to many of her questions, I couldn't help but feel inspired. When the bell rang, the young men immediately packed up their backpacks with an urgency to go somewhere. But Layla lingered, clearly wanting to learn more.

"Dartmouth sounds amazing." She smiled. "I hope someday I see it in person."

"She's never even left the state," one of the young men announced as he shoved his laptop into its case. He turned to Layla. "Have you even been to the panhandle?"

"No, but I've been to Orlando," she offered as an option before turning back to me. "I'll travel out of state someday. But I keep busy here."

"Well, here seems like a perfectly good place to keep busy," I said politely as I packed up my own pile of brochures.

"It's nowheresville," one young man said.

"It's not nowheresville. Tonight, the school's putting on *West Side Story*." Layla shrugged before turning to me. "It's supposed to be good. You should come if you're around."

Another boy swung his backpack over his shoulder as he turned to Layla. "I'm sure she has better things to do."

"It sounds lovely," I said to Layla. "But I have another event tonight near the mall."

Layla lit up. "You can find the best Cuban food right behind the mall. Do you like Cuban food?"

"I've had fried plantains . . ."

"Just fried plantains? There's SO much more to Cuban food than fried plantains. You've got to try a Frita. And Cuban rice and beans. They're spicier than Mexican rice and beans but less salty than Spanish rice and beans. I can give you some recommendations for restaurants while you're here. The possibilities for a great meal are endless."

"She knows everything about food," the remaining young man muttered as he approached me. "But I'm trying to learn everything about history. I'm applying early decision and hope to be one of your history majors someday."

"Terrific." I smiled politely while secretly terribly uninterested.

"I'm Greg," he said as he outstretched his hand. "I don't think we have been properly introduced."

A few minutes earlier, I had watched Greg slowly pull a scab from his elbow and fling it toward the garbage. (He had missed.) I took his hand hesitantly. "Hi, Greg."

"I have a few questions about your history major," he continued. Then he inquired about the European history curriculum, the college's history faculty, and the location of the history department. (Every question could have been answered with a quick look at the history department website.) I was relieved when he finally left the room.

"Greg's really into history," Layla said. "I gave him a book to read last year about William Howard Taft, since he's the only other person besides me who I thought would enjoy it."

"That was kind of you," I said. "Are you interested in history as well?"

"I'm interested in everything."

"Including food, obviously," I added. "Are you an aspiring chef?"

"Nah." She laughed. "I'm just interested in the *people* who make the food." She wrote down a few words with her pencil on a piece of lined paper. "There's this one guy, Daniel, who runs his own restaurant. He has the most amazing stories about growing up in Ethiopia. And if you like Thai food, my friend Samson has a food truck that serves *to-die-for* basil chicken. And then there's June, whose family recipes were handed down by memory since most of her relatives were illiterate."

"You know a lot of characters."

"I want to be a fiction writer someday. These characters will inspire my characters."

Layla and I chatted for a few more minutes until her counselor interrupted us. He didn't remember Layla's name but was sure to put a plug in for Greg, "the standout swimmer on his team." (He spoke over Layla as if she were invisible.)

Having not much interest in talking to the counselor (who already annoyed me in an earlier introduction when he called me "a gal who didn't look like she came from New Hampshire"),* I focused my attention back on Layla. Before leaving, she handed me a paper filled with restaurant recommendations. "I hope next time I see you it will be on your campus."

"I hope so, too. Until then, study hard."

"I hardly *study*, Mrs. Sabky." She flashed a knowing smile. "I just pay attention."

People often asked me what made an applicant memorable in person. "You know it when you see it," I'd reply. But the truth was that I didn't see it often.

The students I remembered sometimes weren't memorable for the right reasons. Like the young person who blurted out "state sexuals" three times to me in conversation instead of "state sectionals" (before running out of the room in embarrassment).† Or the straight-faced

---

* What does that mean, anyway?

† This, rightly or unjustly, will forever be my most vivid memory of working in college admissions.

young man who asked me how much money his father would need to donate for his admission. Or the young woman who loudly chewed chili cheese fries while I was presenting.

As terrible as it is to admit, "perfection" in students had become mundane. Everyone was an accomplished painter, a drum major, or a soccer MVP. Everyone had achieved an A in honors American literature. Everyone was achieving, scoring, and accomplishing.

These young people were incredible. It was a privilege to meet them. But the thing that most impressed me in person was *the* person. It wasn't an honor, a trophy, or a grade. (With a self-selecting pool at Dartmouth, nearly all the students we met were strong students.) Instead, I was taken with the way the person acted among his peers, respected his community, and treated others.

The most impressive students I met on the road:

1. Led with their person, not their accolades. (I'd eventually learn Ben won the county debate championships. He didn't need to bang me over the head with it.)

2. Asked questions with ungoogleable answers. (Admissions officers like to be more valuable than the pamphlets they carry.)

3. Acted as ambassadors for their schools. (An officer will be grateful to learn exactly why Peter Rabbit High School is known for its French program.)

4. Celebrated (instead of competing with) their peers. (There is nothing uglier than watching students one-up each other in the hope of getting ahead.)

I remembered students with authentic passion in their voices. (I closed down a Tennessee auditorium an hour after a session because I was so enamored with the way a young man talked about his pride for his mother.) I was touched by students who welcomed me to and informed me about their community. (A self-described introverted student convinced me that her hometown was relevant because of its proximity to both north, south, east, and westbound trains. She was admitted to Dartmouth and never stopped exploring campus and beyond. Although she was quieter than others in our exchanges, her few words were meaningful.) I was excited by students who weren't afraid to laugh, engage, and be vulnerable. (One young woman in Colorado graciously pointed out the poppyseed stuck in my tooth, despite dozens of others who hadn't had the nerve.)

Our office didn't expect (or encourage) us to keep notes on the students whom we met on the road. (Interestingly, Dartmouth admissions officers were required to keep detailed notes on *schools** we visited in a shared database, as this information was crucial in planning from year to year.) I'd check off a roster of students who attended my events (so that they would receive demonstrated interest credit), but I wasn't expected to comment on them. Occasionally, I would comment if:

There was something out of the ordinary to say. ("*Bruce was the student at the school visit who publicly shot down the others for laughing at our Lesbian, Gay, Bisexual, and Transgender Studies program.*")

There was something important to add. ("*The receptionist in the lobby whispered to me that Cheryl was the favorite among not only faculty, but also the staff.*")

There was an impression worth preserving. ("*Casey asked for an extra brochure at the end of the presentation. She's been collecting them for her cousin 'whose college resources aren't as substantial' at a nearby high school.*)

---

* Embarrassingly, I also remembered details that didn't matter: which school was closest to In-N-Out Burger, which school gave me a parking ticket, which school offered the best Halloween candy in the main office. I kept these all-important details in an offline private notebook.

Not everyone had the chance to make an impression on me. (It was unfair. It was complicated. And it was a reality of competitive admissions.) Not everyone realized that often the behavior that left the biggest impression happened outside of the counseling office. (While quietly walking behind two prospective students on a sidewalk of one of the country's most competitive private high schools, I overheard them discussing their weekend "Thong Pong" tournament. When we arrived at the counseling office, their college counselor introduced them to me as the school's "best and brightest." The moment still haunts me.) And even my endorsement of a student wouldn't confirm admission. (A few of my "favorites" were denied annually.) Admissions was a business, and even my word could move an applicant only so far.

But it felt decent to vouch for a person's curiosity and/or kindness. (I estimate I commented on only about a dozen applicants annually.) I knew the kindest kid in the world still wouldn't be admitted if his grades were poor. I knew that the most impressive applicant in person would still have to complete a strong paper application. But I also knew that endorsing a few students made the job more palatable, more humane, more bearable. And when my commentary on character and/or behavior helped to push a student over the hump (like when I vouched for a young man whose sense of humor eased the tension in the room at a high-achieving high school), I felt a renewed passion for the job.

There's no way a student can ensure he'll wow an admissions officer during a visit. (If there was, it would take away the authenticity of human relationships.) And since some admissions officers don't keep detailed notes on the students they meet on the road, even a wonderful interaction might not make much of a difference in the admissions process. But a prospective student should still extend himself to his specific admissions officer. He should tell the officer a little something special about his school, his community, or himself. And he should make his interest in the college clear.

For example, a student who met an admissions officer might jog her memory:

Dear Mrs. Sabky,

It was lovely meeting with you at Mira High School last week.
If you recall, I was the student who arrived first to the meeting.
We talked about our mutual habits of arriving early to
presentations and joked about being first to our own funerals.

Dartmouth continues to be a top college choice, and after
learning about your history department, I booked a ticket to visit
in November. Until then, I'll be continuing to arrive early to
photography club. (As the early bird, I always earn first dibs in
the darkroom.)

Best, Annie Wynne

Or she might simply summon an admissions officer's attention:

Dear Ms. Sabky,

My name is Paula Stonehouse, and I'm currently a junior at
Fern High School in Fernwood, New Jersey. I'm sorry that
you won't have the chance to visit Fern High School this fall.
I hope you consider a visit in the spring as I would love for you
to get to know my school and its students. We're known for our
marching band, which is currently practicing for the Macy's
Thanksgiving Day Parade, our incredible physics department,
and our award-winning baking club (of which I'm president
and lead taste tester).

I'm disappointed that I won't be able to meet you in person.
But I'm happy to let you know that Dartmouth is currently
one of my top college choices. (I'm considering applying early
decision next year.) I hope you have a wonderful trip to New
Jersey, and I hope our paths cross soon. (And if you need a travel
suggestion, I highly recommend a lighthouse tour on the Jersey
shore.)

Safe travels, Paula

These e-mails are helpful because they are specific. They allow an officer a glimpse into the personality of the writer. And they don't require lengthy responses from the receiver.

Most importantly, they provide a paper trail of student-admissions engagement. Many offices will upload relevant e-mails directly into an applicant's application to be reread during review. Since admissions officers don't often document students they meet, it helps if a student documents his own existence.

The bottom line is that most competitive colleges are aggressively recruiting off campus to drum up more applications. (The more applications, the more competitive admissions rate. The more competitive admissions rate, the more "elite" they're considered. The more "elite" they're considered, the more attractive to prospective students. The more attractive, the more selective. The cycle continues.) Simultaneously, students are trying to win the attention of these admissions officers to stand out in these growing pools. The juxtaposition of these goals is ironic, silly, and frustrating.

Many competitive colleges don't *need* to recruit more applicants. Most already have a diverse pool, chock-full of talent, with ridiculously competitive admissions rates. (One could argue that they need to further diversify their pools, but in that sense, they would have shifted recruitment to focus on schools with diverse student bodies, rather than continuing to recruit students from the same select schools year after year.) But they *want* more applications to keep up with the Cornells. (We monitored the number of applicants and, more importantly, the selection rate of our fellow Ivy League schools closely.)

Personally, I wondered if competitive colleges should stop driving in circles and permanently park our cars. I thought we should stop hunting for underrepresented students and start thinking more thoughtfully about how to serve these students on campus. I believed we should stop hobnobbing with high-ranking high schools for our own gratification and start visiting schools with more diverse cars in their parking lots. I hoped we would stop pulling students out of class as we professed the importance of education.

But travel had its upside: it made me a better admissions officer. It helped me witness firsthand the country's disparity among school resources. (Some schools offered gender-inclusive bathrooms with free hygiene products; others were missing stall doors and had floating cigarettes in the toilet water.) It permitted me to observe high schoolers in their natural surroundings. (I always learned more about the school community in the hallways than I did in the classrooms.) It helped me understand the distance traveled by students on their path to education. (Some school counselors seemed more worried about lost pens than lost freshmen.) And it allowed me to talk *to* students (rather than just about students).

College admissions offices spend a lot of time and money on recruitment travel. A student may as well take advantage of events in his neighborhood. He should attend public information sessions. He should inquire about nearby college fairs. He should reach out to a regional admissions officer and invite him to visit his school. (Why not be your own school advocate in a recruiting system of such inequality?) And he should do his best to engage with the human who flew seven hundred miles to sit in his cafeteria during study hall.

But he should also know that admissions officers are human. They tire of perfection. They're rooting for the poppy-seed-in-the-tooth pointers. They're often more impressed by the Laylas than the valedictorians. And often, even they can't get someone admitted.

Of the tens of thousands of students I met on the road, Layla is the most memorable. But she's also the one that got away.* She never applied to the college. I never heard from her (or about her) again. I never had the chance to comment on her curiosity or kindness.

---

* One of my greatest professional regrets is not following up after our school visit to encourage her application. I just *assumed* she'd be in the pool.

I'm not confident that Layla would have been admitted, even if she had applied. (I never saw her scores or transcript.) But she set the bar for what I was looking for in other applicants. She redefined to me what it meant to be "impressive." And she was the student who I knew would be successful whatever her postsecondary path.

THE APPLICATION

CHAPTER SIX

THE SCHOOL REPORT

As students progressed further in the college admissions search, they thought more critically about how their eventual applications would be reviewed by admissions offices. The two most popular questions I received from prospective students were:

"Is it better to receive a B in an AP class or an A in an honors class?"

and

"Is it better to be ranked tenth at a competitive private school or first at a less-competitive public high school?"

There were no easy answers to these specific questions. But the questioners essentially were asking the same thing: Did admissions officers consider the context of a student's academic career? And the answer was a firm YES.

Many families have questions about how particular high schools and curriculums are viewed in the eyes of an admissions committee. They want to know if colleges favor schools that offer AP classes or schools that offer IB curriculums. (At Dartmouth and many other competitive colleges, it didn't matter.) They want to know if STEM schools give an advantage to students pursuing engineering. (Not necessarily.) They want to know if there is a "best" high school to prepare one for college. (Hogwarts rules.) They want to know how to best position a student for admission.

"The reason I'm asking"—the mother on the phone cut me off—"is because Michael has the choice between Butternut Prep or Hickory High. I thought I'd reach out to Dartmouth for advice before we commit to either school."

"And he's currently in *eighth* grade?" I confirmed over the phone.

"Yes. But we want to position him in the best possible way for college success four years from now."

I remained neutral as I spoke. "Unfortunately, we can't advise students on school choice. I'm sure he'd do fine at either school. We admit students from both."

My answer was unacceptable. She pressed on. "Okay then, which school gets more kids into Dartmouth?"

"I can't share that information."

"I'm sure it's Butternut Prep. But then again, I think he'd stand out more at Hickory High." She sweetened her voice as she spoke. "I know that you're not allowed to favor one school over the other. But off the record, just between you and me, where would you send him if he were your kid?"

I wished that her son was the person who had picked up the phone. (While it's fine for parents to be appropriately involved in the college process, it was better when an actual applicant advocated for his candidacy.) Regardless, I wasn't going to tell the mother or her son that my most unlikable college peer (who once heckled me for wearing tapered jeans) was a proud Butternut Prep graduate. But I'd also heard that Hickory High recently cut its arts and music programs due to lack of funding. I personally preferred Middle of the Road Academy, a third option in a neighboring county, with incredible language programs, generous financial aid policies, and a more diverse student body. But of course I couldn't say so. (I didn't want to be accused of or sued for favoritism discrimination.) And, frankly, my opinion didn't matter. We were urged to read without school bias.

"I'd send him where he wants to go."

"That's what I was afraid you'd say." The mother laughed. "He doesn't know where he wants to go. The schools are so different."

She was right. The schools were different. I wasn't very sympathetic to her plight (most people I knew would be thrilled to have the problem), but I did understand her dilemma.

Experienced admissions officers become experts on high schools. I've walked the halls of hundreds of preps, academies, highs, techs, and magnets. I know which schools welcome students with granola-bar-filled goody bags upon arrival and which ones require metal detection upon entrance. I've spent significant time at large schools and small schools, mountain schools and island schools, schools of the rich and schools of the poor.

And what I learned over the years is that students are admitted to Dartmouth and other competitive colleges from *everywhere*. They come from manicured private schools, conservative parochial schools, middle-of-rural-North-Dakota homeschools, underfunded inner-city schools, and semiprofessional tennis academies. Every student at every school is given a shot at admission.

But there are a few schools with an advantage on that shot. These are select schools with experienced, informed, and well-connected college counselors. These schools tend to cost top dollar to afford "college counselor" rather than just "school counselor" positions. Counselors at these schools are experienced in the business of college admissions and know how a student can best (legally) present an application. They know to urge school administrators to diminish school rank. (Rank often doesn't help students at competitive schools where many are fighting for the top of their class.) They're well versed in the advantages of early decision programs. (Many face pressures from their own schools to place students in the most "elite" institutions.) And they have the direct phone numbers of their regional admissions officer.

In my opinion, "counselor calls" were the secret handshake of the privileged counselor. In mid-March before college admissions decisions were released, many college admissions officers conducted "counselor calls" with a handful of select high schools to discuss their applicants' probable outcomes. (Dartmouth was in good company making these calls with many other competitive colleges and universities.) Colleges argue that these calls strengthen relationships with "trusted" high schools. Counselors making these calls argue that this is a time to provide any updated information (such as midterm grades) and to receive lead time to prepare for tough family conversations with the denied. I argue that these calls are nothing more than an insider's privilege.

The ick factor of these calls is obvious. To begin, we didn't have the time to speak to every counselor in our assigned territory, but we'd make time for schools in the know that requested these calls. Secondly, giving admissions decisions secretly to anyone other than the actual applicant felt dishonorable. (As far as I was concerned, Jane Doe should be the first to know Jane Doe's admissions decision, not her counselor.) Above all, these calls could influence admissions decisions. If a student's application status was not yet decided, a counselor could try to persuade an admissions officer of an admit. It was unfair to other applicants who didn't have the same advocacy and, in my opinion, ethically questionable since we couldn't be sure if a counselor's advocacy was solely based on a student's merit. While I very much enjoyed working with most of the calling counselors and recognized the pressures they were facing on the other side of the desk, I couldn't help but wonder if a few were taking advantage of the opportunity. (Luckily for us, if all colleges agree to stop the madness, counselor calls are easy to abolish.)

Most American high school students don't have this type of advocacy.* Most students report to a *school* (not college) counselor who is responsible for three hundred students whose last names start with

---

* According to the National Center for Education Statistics, approximately 90 percent of American high school students attended public schools in 2015. While there are wonderful college counselors at many public high schools in this country, I found that most counselors who could afford the time to go the extra mile for their students came from private schools. Many public school counselors (though well intentioned) appeared to be spread too thin.

M–Z. These counselors likely don't know the name of their regional representative. (Some might not know the first names of the students they counsel.) These counselors can be as busy with detention duty as they are with SAT registration. And these counselors are almost always overworked (and often underpaid).

As a product of a suburban public school, I understand the challenges of applying to colleges from less-resourced schools. While I did fine academically, my high school didn't do much to inspire my learning. During those four years, I learned curse words from the graffiti on the bathroom walls. A few of my teachers were mediocre, at best.* I didn't take a single science class my senior year due to scheduling difficulties. But my journey to college wasn't as severe as others. (As a white, upper-middle-class woman born to college-educated parents, I was privileged when it came to educational opportunities.)

We'll never know if I would have thrived at the fancy private school up the street. I might have crumbled there under peer pressure. (I'm not sure my tendency toward Samba soccer sneakers would have been appreciated by the loafer-wearing crowd.) I might not have been a standout academically. (I'm sure my class ranking would not have been as strong.) I'm not sure the college counselor could have convinced an admissions committee to admit me (particularly among a more competitive peer group).

But what I do know is that most students don't have the choice of where to spend their four years of secondary school. Some students face enormous hurdles as they attempt to navigate the process from under-resourced communities, schools, and families. Others choose schools based on social interests, the diversity of the class, athletic recruitment, proximity, or financial opportunities. While colleges were allowing counselors with privilege to speak to us on the phone, we also were doing our best to read every applicant in context of his schooling.

---

* One of my teachers inspired me to become a writer. He was one of the hardest graders in the school, but he forced me to care about dangling participles and the overuse of the word "actually." He *actually* made a big impact on me.

A student privileged enough to make a choice about where he attends high school should go to the school that will best educate him. While there are some schools with more dedicated college counseling offices, a student worrying about which school "will get him into the best college" is missing the point. (After exposing the unfairness of counselor calls, I also hope that this practice will quickly become irrelevant.) The point is to make the most of any opportunity to learn, to grow, to mature. Colleges don't expect everyone to attend fancy schools, but they do expect them to make the most of their experience.

"You've probably never heard of my high school," Jasmine said as she took a bite of her burger at our Faculty Friday luncheon event. (On certain summer Fridays, our office invited prospective students to listen to a faculty member wax poetic about his academic subject. After the program, we'd offer them a burger and potato chips at a courtyard picnic near the office.)

"Try me." I smiled over my relish-smothered burger.

"Bananarama High."

"In Michigan?"

"Yep," she said, surprised by my knowledge.

"I've heard of it." I smiled. "But I've never visited."

"There's not much to see." She laughed as she put down her burger. "It's not a good school or anything."

"There must be something good about it."

She paused for a moment. "We've got a good hockey team. The girls, not the guys. I think they won states this year." She popped a potato chip in her mouth.

"Anything else?" I pressed.

"The cafeteria just added hot bagels to the lunch options. They're pretty decent."

"So, hockey and bagels. What about the academics?"

"They're average at best. It's not like we're Uptown Prep."

"Uptown Prep?"

"I'm *sure* you know Uptown Prep," she said dramatically.

"I've heard of it." I nodded. "It's a good school in Ann Arbor, right?"

"It's a great school in Ann Arbor," she said. "All the smart kids go there."

"Not *all* the smart kids."

She smirked through silence.

I took a bite of my burger. "Now, tell me more about *your* school. There's got to be at least one decent teacher."

"Mr. Smalls," she answered. "He's the only one who gets me."

"Then tell me about Mr. Smalls and what he 'gets.'"

Students like Jasmine are a dime a dozen in college admissions. They go to schools they don't believe can compete with the fancy-pants privates. They don't receive the college counseling resources available at schools that prioritize "going Ivy." But the truth is that every student can compete in the admissions process, regardless of where one goes to high school. Some just need to do a little more legwork. *

Their legwork begins with understanding how to contextualize their academic experience to an admissions committee. Most high school students don't visit other high schools. They don't realize that not every curriculum requires four years of language or a full senior semester of Parallel Parking 101. They don't recognize that unweighted rank hurts students taking challenging academic classes and weighted rank (typically) penalizes students for loving arts electives. But in order to present their best applications, they need to provide a clear frame of reference of their own academic history.

On most college applications (including the Common Application), one's academic history is reported through three components.

---

* Nope, it's not fair. Let's work on changing the system. Go!

1. The Transcript

Transcripts are fairly straightforward. ("A" grades look good. "F" grades look bad.) In my experience, admissions officers view entire transcripts (and not just GPAs) looking at trends, classes, and individual grades. (A few school transcripts include standardized and state testing results, AP test scores, and teacher comments on behavior.) Reading a transcript isn't difficult. But understanding a transcript in context of a school's offerings can be. This is where the high school profile comes in handy . . .

2. The High School Profile

The high school profile is a document rarely seen or discussed by college-bound students. There's nothing secretive about it (as most schools publish them on their own websites). But often students haven't seen their own high school profiles (or heard of them) before they are submitted by their counseling office with their transcript. Yet a high school profile can be critical in the admissions review process as it typically contains:

a. **An explanation of the grading system.** (At Mercury High, honors classes are weighted on a 5.0 scale; regular classes are weighted on a 4.0 scale.)

b. **An overview of classes offered and any relevant curriculum policies.** (Although Venus High School offers fifteen AP classes, students are prohibited from taking more than a total of five over four years.)

c. **Graduation requirements.** (All young women at Saturn Girls Academy must pass Debutante Ball Etiquette* before receiving their diplomas.)

From there, the profiles vary. Some profiles share the fancy degrees awarded to administrators. ("*Our headmaster went to Harvard, our*

---

* I've seen some crazy classes out there, folks.

school nurse went to Yale, and our chief vegan compliance officer went to Princeton.") Some profiles boast a long list of colleges attended by the school's previous class. (*"Seven students in our senior class were admitted to Palm Tree University in the Class of 2021."*) Some list academically irrelevant information. (*"Our school mascot is the red Teletubby. Go Teletubbies!"*)

Regardless of how well done or how thorough, the profile serves as the map key for any admissions officer reviewing a transcript. Applicants need to know what their schools are telling (and not telling) colleges so that they can fill in the blanks with an additional letter. (Stay tuned!)

3. The Counselor Recommendation

As admissions officers, we recognized that not every applicant knew her counselor well. (We expected teacher recommendations to go to bat for an applicant. But we understood that counselor relationships could vary.) Still, the counselor recommendation was required as an overview of a student's three-and-a-half-year performance. (Parents of home-schooled students can write counselor recommendations if they are the best folks to comment on a student's overall academic work.) At best, we would hope that a counselor could provide insight on a student's curriculum choices, motivations, and school-wide influences not otherwise available in the application. (*"While she won't be valedictorian this year, Caroline was chosen by the yearbook staff as "Class Intellectual," a nod to her classmates' respect for her mind, regardless of her rank."*) At worst, a counselor would waive the letter, noting that his workload was too time-consuming for college counseling. (Unfortunately, this happened a few times every year.) Most college recommendations were somewhere in between.

I advise students to schedule a meeting with the counselor assigned to their college application as early as possible (and certainly by junior spring). The more a student extends himself to the writer of the counselor recommendation, the more helpful to the writer, and (hopefully) the better the recommendation. I also encourage students to have a conversation with the counselor about pertinent information that a student might hope to be included in his school report: *"Mr. Flay, I'm concerned colleges won't understand my decision to switch languages from Japanese to French mid-sophomore year. Do you think this is something you could speak to in your letter?"*

Once a student understands what's being submitted by his school, he can better understand what (if necessary) still needs to be contextualized. Regardless of whether he goes to a school lined with oriental carpets or metal detectors, a student has the power to self-advocate for his own academic experience. But most students don't know that they *can*.

There is no section on an application asking a student to comment on his school report. Admissions committees don't seek out these letters. But sending an additional letter (or using the "Additional Information" section on the Common Application) can be helpful if there's something relevant to include. As a possible example:

Dear Admissions Committee,
Give me a Bunsen burner and I'm comfortable. Give me a
graphing calculator and I thrive. But put me on a stage and
I shrivel.
    As a junior, I decided to go out on a limb and take
Introduction to Theater Arts as an elective during my regular
study-hall period. I wanted to challenge myself, as public
speaking has always been a weakness. I met with the teacher
twice a week for extra help. I spent weeks memorizing my fear-
inducing monologue. And I spent many more hours than I'd like
to admit on practicing "tears" in the mirror.
    The class was superbly difficult for me. I earned a B-. It's the
lowest grade on my transcript, but the proudest grade of my life.
    While I'll never win an Oscar, the class helped me find my

voice. I have confidence now to speak up when it matters. (In a few days, I plan on mustering up the courage to ask the special someone to prom.) The class changed me for the better, and although I'll be returning to my Bunsen burner, I'll never forget lessons from the stage.

Sincerely yours, Martin

I encouraged students to submit a brief letter to the admissions committee sharing relevant insight on academic performance, if applicable. (In Martin's case, his letter confirmed his motivations, his ability to step outside of his comfort zone, and his personality.) I assured them they could share anything on their minds. Even if it seemed technical. (*Our high school doesn't offer credit for community college courses, so my advanced math grade is not included in my GPA calculation.*) Even if it seemed to dwell on minutiae. (*While my profile mentions AP German, it wasn't offered this year as it didn't attract enough seniors.*) Even if it seemed trivial. (*Mrs. Stoneface is the hardest grader in the school who hasn't given an A in twenty-three years.*)

In my career, I had dozens of conversations with students worried about grades and curriculum choices. They obsessed about their competitiveness if they took a class outside of the standard five subjects. (The big five were classes in science, English, history, language, and math.) They hemmed and hawed about classes that would give them an admissions edge. (*"Will taking environmental science stand out more than taking anatomy?"*) They sacrificed their interests (improv) for what they thought would look good (Latin). But instead of theorizing on what academic track might help them get admitted, they'd best consider which track would prepare them for college and beyond.

Admissions offices didn't want to crush one's academic pursuits. We just needed to know that a student had challenged himself in high school, was prepared for the rigors of a college classroom, and proved hungry to learn more. We were flexible with underclass grades, particularly if a student had an "upward trend" during his upperclassman years.

(Senior-year midyears carried far more weight than freshman grades.) We were encouraging of meaningful electives, providing that a student had a strong base for the rigors of a college classroom. (Hello! Arts and electives are critical in our classrooms!) * And while we loved seeing AP, IB, and honors classes on a transcript, we weren't going to hold it against a student if he took a class (or three) without one of these distinctions, providing he told us *why*.

Making an admissions officer's job easier (especially when it comes to understanding a transcript) is always smart. I was thrilled when a student (or counselor) pointed out the wonky math behind an honors-unfriendly GPA calculation. I was impressed when Casey defended her curriculum choice to stick with the language arts track over the STEM track despite the school's urging. I was relieved to hear that April chose regular-tracked Chinese over AP French because she hoped to better communicate with her cousins in Shanghai. These letters not only helped provide insight on a candidate; they made the admissions officer's job easier.

I'm not arguing that students must write letters defending their lowest grades on their transcripts. I'm not encouraging folks to whine about teachers who are tough graders. (Mrs. Stoneface, who hasn't given an A in twenty-three years, is the exception.) And I'm certainly not requesting students complete the Additional Information section with repetitive information just to fill space. But I am making the case for a student to speak up about her high school experience if there's something to say.[†] And there's often *something* to say.

---

* Admissions offices often discussed our role in encouraging the arts as valued academic subjects, particularly in a time of budget cuts in these disciplines.

† I wish I had told the admissions committee when I was applying to college that I was proud of being a graduate of my high school, despite its average academic record. I wish I had told them that it was good for me to ride the bus for forty minutes each way with students from different backgrounds and interests. (Some days, I learned more on that bus than I did all day at school.) I wish I had told them that I enjoyed taking public speaking with my younger sister, even though she achieved a better grade.

"Ask her," the mother encouraged her daughter. "Go ahead. Just ask her."

The young woman took a deep breath before speaking up. "I want to make room in my schedule for a vocal class. But if I take that class, I won't be able to double up on math in the fall."

Her mother didn't wait for my answer. "Kelly needs to double up on math to be competitive out of her high school."

I looked at Kelly. "Have you taken a vocal class before?"

"Never. In middle school, I was stuck in the band track because they needed a female drummer. But I always wanted to sing."

"And do you know if you want to major in math in college?"

She laughed. "Definitely not."

Her mother inserted herself. "She wants to be a history professor."

"Then take the vocal class."

The mother looked at me, disappointed. "Instead of AP Statistics? It will hurt her weighted rank."

"What's the other math class you're taking?" I turned to Kelly.

"AP Calculus."

"Take the vocal class," I repeated. "And if you're worried how it looks, write to us and explain why you made your choice."

"Then she'll only have four AP classes and her peers will have five."

"She'll still be viewed as a bright young lady with all of those APs," I insisted.

"A bright young lady"—Kelly paused—"who *finally* learned to sing."

A person's experience in high school shouldn't just be about college admissions probability. Students shouldn't just take classes in their predictable wheelhouse. Students should take classes that will enlighten, challenge, and inspire them. Students should read *Beloved*, memorize the periodic table, and write that paper about the Mexican-American War, rather than obsessing over how their classes "look" to admissions committees. Students should take responsibility for their own educations and defend the heck out of their choices. Students shouldn't make excuses, but they should make their case.

Would an admissions committee rather a student receive a B in an AP class than an A in an honors class? Maybe. Is Michael more advantaged in the admissions process as a middle-of-the-pack student at a highly competitive high school or a standout student at a less-resourced school? Possibly. Is a student with seven honors courses and an elective in music disadvantaged in the admissions process over a student with eight honors classes? Perhaps.

The answers to these questions depend on the *why*. The results are based on the *reasoning*. An applicant's *outcome* is determined by an applicant's *input*.

A student's schooling and curriculum decisions (if lucky enough to choose) shouldn't be based on what "looks good" to a committee, but rather what "is good" for him. By best educating his person, he's best positioning himself for any college, any job, any future. And in my experience, no admissions office will ever penalize a student for taking a music class if her heart longs to sing.

CHAPTER SEVEN

RECOMMENDATIONS

A letter of recommendation matters in the college admissions process. It can confirm that the valedictorian isn't a narcissist. It can argue that the student with a B+ in French is more intellectually curious than another student with an A. It can ensure that a student's imagination, willingness to take risks, and humility equal her outstanding grade point average. Best of all, it can offer an admissions reviewer something that doesn't exist on a transcript.

At Dartmouth, we received three recommendations for every applicant. In my estimation, I read approximately forty thousand letters in my career. But the greatest and most helpful recommendation I read was written by a member of a school's custodial staff. (I wrote about this letter in an April 2017 *New York Times* op-ed entitled "Check This Box if You're a Good Person.") The janitor had volunteered to write the letter on behalf of the applicant because that student was the only young person who had ever bothered to learn his name. He praised an applicant for simple but often forgotten acts, such as picking up trash in the hallways and bothering to learn staff members' names. He commented on the student's academic reputation around the school. But his greatest endorsement was for the kindness of the young person.

This recommendation revealed something a transcript couldn't capture. It elevated a student's candidacy by offering an anecdote we hadn't heard from other applicants. And it spoke to the student's heart in addition to his mind.

A recommendation from a custodian doesn't call for automatic admission. Admissions is still a business that needs to balance and produce a carefully crafted class. But when all tangible qualities are equal, a recommendation that sheds light on a student's intellectual and personal qualities can help to nudge an application to the admit bin.

The main recommendations required in college applications are from teachers. Teacher recommendations often contribute to a *holistic* admissions review. (A holistic review means using all sections of an application to balance and understand a student's whole candidacy.) Without these letters, a student's academic profile would be strictly numeric. The way a student *thinks* would matter less than the number on a transcript.

Common Application teacher recommendations are comprised of two components: the ratings box and a letter. In the ratings box, teachers are asked to "rate" their students in a series of academic and personal qualifications (i.e., quality of writing, concern for others, integrity, self-confidence). Some teachers checked the "top 1 percent" on multiple applicants' boxes, leading to ratings inflation. (It was hard to believe that an experienced chemistry teacher had seven of the "best of his career" students in a single class.) Some teachers were more conservative (and appropriate) in their box checking. But the extremes of how teachers used these boxes nearly voided their usefulness. (In my opinion, it was unfair to ask teachers to pit students against one another with numerical percentages.)* Most admissions officers relied on the content of a recommendation letter far more than the ratings box.

The recommendation letter prompt itself asks teachers to share "whatever is important." Teachers are encouraged to contextualize a student's classroom behavior. And they're given the freedom to say anything relevant to a student's candidacy.

Most teachers aren't trained on how to write helpful college recommendations. But every so often, a recommendation captures something lovely. A sentiment about behavior out of class: *"The only young man who helped me shovel out of the parking lot."* A note on performance: *"The*

---

* Some savvy schools created policy to prohibit the use of the ratings box in college recommendations. If I were a headmaster, I'd likely do the same.

young woman who allows others their turn to speak, even though she knows the answers." A comment on dignity: *"The only student employed by the school's fields and grounds department, who tirelessly paints lines on the sports fields after the players have gone home."* These were the lines we'd recite on our summary cards, the details we'd highlight from the laundry list of activities and honors, the traits that caught our attention. (My attention was also captured by humor: *"Sure, he needs a good hair brushing, but the boy knows the periodic table."*)

I'd always wished we could offer more teacher recommendation training. But any teacher could get a point across if she spoke about something other than the numbers. The best letters:

1. Were specific.
They used pointed adjectives. (They avoided words like "great" and "smart" but instead used words like "plucky" and "versatile.") They used descriptive comparisons to describe a student. (Describing an applicant as the *"Julia Child of the chemistry lab"* is a brilliant observation.) They offered character confirmation. (*"Michelle is the student I would choose to sit next to on a school trip."*) And they didn't waste time on irrelevant matters. (A teacher once boasted that a student achieved the highest schoolwide score on a popular video game without giving any evidence of why she believed this mattered.)

2. Reframed superlatives.
Although one student had the highest grade point average, the "best student" in the class may have been the student with the sharpest critical mind. (With the exception being French school recommendations where everyone was average and on par. We'd account for their conservatism of praise.)

3. Told us something new.
Although it was clear from her application that Natalie received strong grades in both the humanities and STEM, it was helpful to know that

she was attempting to bridge poetry and computer science in an innovative senior project.

But most importantly, the best recommendation told the student's best story.

"He was so talented, academically and otherwise." The woman shook her head as she spoke to me. "I never met a mind like his."

I was visiting a high school on recruitment, and as I waited in the lobby of the counseling office, a woman had struck up a conversation. She wasn't describing a student I could recruit. She was describing "*oh, what the heck was his name*" from two classes prior. He apparently would have been a great candidate for Dartmouth's engineering school due to his hands-on approach.

"It was just such a small thing, but it's what I remember most about him. He just took his time, working link by link, desperate to untangle the necklace." She laughed. "Near the end of the year, he had every girl in his class giving him their tangled jewelry."

"*Oh, what the heck was his name*" was a math star and an engineering genius at the high school I was visiting. But it was his noncredit work that stood out to this woman. According to her, he was obsessed with using physics and geometry to design a fine jewelry chain that wouldn't tangle.

"He was determined to become an inventor," she said fondly. "His mother used to tell me that he'd tinker away on her jewelry during their car rides to school. Even today, when I put on a necklace, I think of him."

I found myself playing with the chain around my neck. "Do you remember where he went to college?"

"I don't really remember. All I know is that of all the students that went to this school, he's the one I'll never forget."

"I'm sure the college admissions committees loved hearing about his necklace talent."

"His necklace talent?" she huffed. "Oh, honey, admissions committees don't care about that sort of stuff. I'm sure they cared more about his grades. I think he graduated as salutatorian, or at least close."

The necklace story was likely the only thing that would have resonated with an admissions committee. If a recommender wrote that Mr. Necklace was talented and one of the school's best students, it would sound like every other recommendation. But if she wrote that he used his classroom learning for other (interesting) endeavors, it would confirm his intellectual passion.

I wasn't surprised that the woman didn't see the importance of this story. There was so much pressure on people to write recommendations but little feedback on what made a recommendation stand out among the many. It was hard for recommenders to know what mattered.

What made a good recommendation was the same thing that made a great essay, a great interview, a great application: an insight into an applicant's *humanity*. We knew a student's grades. We knew his test scores. But what we didn't know was how he used his mind for good. How he behaved when he believed both everybody and nobody was watching. How he tinkered with necklaces to find a better way.

Of course, students can't write their own recommendations. They can't choose the words written on the page. They can't ensure that a teacher will write what they hope. And they shouldn't be positioning themselves in the classroom only for recommendations. (There's no reason to manufacture teacher relationships.)

Yet building authentic relationships with educators is a useful life tool. Colleges often pride (and market) themselves on their student-faculty relationships. ("Take a Professor to Lunch" is a Dartmouth offering we spoke about regularly.) High school students who develop teacher-mentor skills are preparing themselves for similar relationships in the future. (In my experience, I wish I had learned the value of professor open office hours earlier in my college career.) A college rec shouldn't be the goal of a student's relationship. It should be a happy side effect.

Of course, when it is time to submit recommendations, there are steps to helping a recommender write her best letter (which, in turn, will strengthen a candidacy).

1. **Choose a recommender who can speak to both intangible and tangible qualities.**

With luck, a student has flourished from the care of many "good" teachers. But applications typically require only two teacher recommendations. A teacher who brings out the best in a student is usually the teacher who brings out the best of a student on paper. These are the people who have identified how a student learns, thereby also knowing more about a student's strengths (and weaknesses). In choosing recommenders, I encouraged students to ask one key question:

Whose teaching has had the most impact on my intellectual growth?

Impactful teachers write impactful recommendations. The recommender doesn't have to be the teacher who gave the highest grade on one's transcript. Sometimes a strong recommendation came from a teacher who gave the lowest grade on one's transcript but spoke to the student's persistence. (I would balance this "lowest grade on the transcript" teacher recommendation with another recommendation from a teacher where the student performed well.) The recommender doesn't have to be the teacher from a student's most difficult class. Instead, the best recommendations come from teachers whose impact sparked authentic interest, not necessarily from the teacher of the class where the student learned the most.

Here are two ways teacher relationships could be described:

Theo entered honors biology with an interest in science. He read the textbook ravenously, worked diligently on his independent research paper, and completed all homework assignments. His teacher guided his success but wasn't the catalyst for his interest. He received an A+ in the class.

Theo entered honors anatomy with the same vigor he brought to biology. While he devoured the lessons and was a leader of class projects, it was Mrs. Henderson who challenged him to think differently about the human body. She recognized that Theo brought a unique passion for math to anatomy class, and therefore assigned him innovative interdisciplinary projects that catapulted his learning. He received an A– in the class.

In this case, the honors anatomy teacher should write the letter. The honors biology teacher would surely write a superlative letter for Theo, but his recommendation would likely read like many others. The anatomy teacher, however, had invested in Theo's intellectual growth. (If she invested time in his learning, she'd likely invest time in his letter.) She'd likely have more interesting and insightful things to say about his learning, his inspirations, and his success.

It's worth noting that some colleges have specific recommender requirements. They might encourage letters from teachers within an intended major discipline (e.g., math recs for engineering students) or letters from junior- or senior-year teachers. The best way to find out a school's policy on recommendations is to ask.

But in my experience at Dartmouth and from speaking to other colleagues, admissions officers don't care who writes the letters. Many admissions officers believe that who writes the recommendation doesn't matter as much as what is said. At Dartmouth, it didn't matter if the chemistry teacher's grammar was awful or if Mrs. Belvidere didn't meet the deadline. (We were forgiving of late materials, especially from teachers.) It didn't matter if the letter came from a ninth-grade teacher, a band teacher, or a parent serving as a homeschool teacher.* All that mattered was that the letters told us something relevant.

---

* We asked that homeschooled students find at least one recommendation from outside the household.

2. **Ask for a recommendation as early as possible and provide relevant updates.**

Writing recommendations is hard work. It requires creative word choices, caffeine, and time away from family. I'm sympathetic to counselors and teachers with a heavy load of requests, particularly junior and senior teachers who become bogged down by these requests. (A teacher friend writes over twenty recommendations for students from his junior honors English class each year.)

It seemed to me that the few mistakes and missed opportunities we'd see in teacher letters came from folks whose writing seemed rushed. (I once read a letter of recommendation for Dartmouth where the teacher gushed at how badly the applicant wanted to go to the University of Massachusetts–Dartmouth. But it would have been heartless to hold it against the student.) It's helpful and important to let teachers know way in advance if one plans on asking for a recommendation. Allowing ample time and consideration for letter writing can benefit a student and provide common courtesy. (A biology teacher might spend more time watching a student dissect owl pellets if she knows she'll need to comment on his in-class behavior someday.)

Schools might have different policies on when students can ask teachers for letters. But if a junior history teacher is inspiring one's learning, it can't hurt to mention to the teacher that a student "might" use him for a college recommendation someday. (Even if a student changes his mind, it would at least be flattering.) For those who ask teachers from previous class years (i.e., sophomore teacher), it's helpful to provide relevant updates after making the request (in person, of course). If it's been a while, a teacher will appreciate a refresher. Here's an example of how a student could provide a relevant update.

> Mrs. Terry,
> Thanks for agreeing to write one of my college recommendations. I'm excited to study science at a liberal arts college, and I thank you for making such an impact on my learning.

I know that most of your students weren't crazy for our owl pellet dissection last year in our biology class. But if I had never dissected the lower jawbone to the pygmy shrew in my pellet, I would have never grown to appreciate the sheer tininess of America's smallest mammal. My interest in pygmy shrews ignited my interest in rodents (much to the dismay of my rat-fearing mother), and I'm currently applying for a summer job at the Bronx Zoo's Mouse House. Whether or not I'm hired, I owe it to your enthusiasm for all things four-legged.

Thanks again for your support, Gus

I also encouraged students to disclose their recommenders to one another. Knowing who else will be writing a recommendation can only help colleagues approach their letters from different perspectives, particularly if the teachers are friendly. (*I think it's great that you're writing one of Gus's letters, Alison. I'm writing about his both peculiar and wonderful interest in shrews and how they led to his Mouse House internship this summer. What are you focusing on?*")

Most of all, I recommend that students share the experience with their educators. It's common courtesy to explain how one finalized her college application list with a teacher. It's only human to buy one's teacher a (decent) cup of coffee and discuss what she likes about each college. A teacher can write with more conviction if she knows the why and how of one's college path. And by speaking about one's road to college, a student might receive insightful advice from a teacher who has watched many fellow students navigate the same path. (Handwritten thank-you notes should be written to every recommender, of course.)

3. **Submit an additional recommendation if it can provide a fresh perspective on one's candidacy.**

If a student believes someone other than a counselor or teacher can speak to his candidacy in a new light, he can certainly submit an additional recommendation. (But use discretion so as to avoid appearing desperate.) At Smith, a parent recommendation is encouraged. At Dartmouth, a peer recommendation is strongly recommended. (Yes, the peer rec was a bit of a marketing ploy. *"We're unique in that we care about what your besties have to say about you."* But it was also an opportunity to learn about relevant family, personal, and social life from a second source.) At any school, an additional recommendation is helpful if it provides a new angle.

The most helpful additional recommendations told stories of students in situations that were previously undiscussed. (For example, the janitor recommendation revealed a student's behavior in the hallway when nobody was watching.) Letters from clergy, coaches, employers, and mentors had the potential to contribute a fresh perspective. An additional letter from a piano teacher might speak to a student's commitment to music. A recommendation from the town police chief might confirm a student's devotion to community. And, of course, I'd advise students not to turn down a letter from someone who is volunteering her support unsolicited. (If a person *insists* on supporting a student's candidacy, she likely will bring her passion to the page.)

However, there is no need to submit a recommendation from someone who doesn't have much to add. It's unnecessary to feel one needs to submit an extra letter from someone "important." (I always argued that a recommendation from an office receptionist who deals with dozens of prospective students daily would mean a lot more to an admissions committee than another headmaster letter.) A letter from Michelle Obama isn't going to be helpful if it's vague. A letter from an alumna family friend is unhelpful unless it offers a new angle on one's candidacy. A letter from a college faculty member is useless unless she goes to bat for a candidate. (I've read faculty letters from folks at Dartmouth and elsewhere who seem to shrug their shoulders and say, "Yep, she'd do.") What matters most is how well the recommender knows the applicant, not how well the admissions committee knows the recommender.

As an admissions director, I looked forward to reading recommendations.* Without recommendations, the race to college would be a much colder process. I was touched by the countless hours our educators sacrificed to help our young people follow their college dreams. And I was thankful when a recommendation shared a detail that helped me argue for one student's admission over similarly accomplished applicants.

But the applicants who had the most to gain from recommendations were the students who had the most to offer. The student who tinkered with jewelry on the way to school. The student who is the teacher's first choice as a bus mate on a school trip. The student who not only pronounced her French vocabulary correctly but also bothered to learn the correct pronunciation of the cafeteria manager's name. (It's A-lee-sha, not A-lish-a.) These were young people with stories. These were applicants with defining details to share. These were the folks I assumed teachers *enjoyed* recommending.

It's great to be a good student. It's wonderful to impress one's teachers. But it's even better to give them something to talk about.

---

* There was one (somewhat overused) line of a teacher recommendation that always caught my eye: "I hope my son grows up to be just like Prospective Student X." It was surely a soppy sentiment. But man, it was my Kryptonite.

CHAPTER EIGHT

EXTRACURRICULARS

Like most other parents, my father had only good intentions. "It will look good on your college résumé," he assured me in high school.

I hated varsity soccer. I hated wearing shin guards. I hated my teammates' obsession with beating Sparta. (*Who had time to care about beating Sparta when the New Kids on the Block were dropping their next album?*) But every day, I dragged myself to practice. For four years I wanted to quit. But the fear of college rejection kept me wearing cleats.

I couldn't blame my dad for encouraging me to stick with the sport. Soccer taught me teamwork, athleticism, and commitment. It made sense that it would help me be admitted to college. Soccer would be the sport that "rounded out" my résumé. It would be more seriously considered than backyard berry picking (my real passion).

There were extracurricular activities I loved for reasons other than the pressures of college. Ski racing was a natural obsession. Working on the yearbook was enjoyable. But being National Honor Society president was about the title. (I did *nothing* as president.) Volunteering with Each One Reach One (an elementary school mentoring club) was solely to check the community service box. (I enjoyed the free lollipops more than time on the playground.) And serving in Spanish Honor Society, well, let's just say, "*Fue solo por apariencia.*" *

Since I wasn't exceptional at any one thing, to get into college I had to be decent at lots of things. Lots and lots of things. As many things as

---

* "It was just for looks."

I could squeeze into a week. Most applicants I met in my career felt the same way.

We were wrong.

I gave a lot of extracurricular advice to prospective students during my time at Dartmouth. I'm not sure everyone was listening to my words. (I wouldn't have believed an admissions officer who told me that quitting high school soccer really wouldn't have any impact on my application.) But I had a lot to say about the topic. I told students to:

1. **Become busy because *you can*, not because *you should*.** High school is the time to experiment, join, quit,* retry, and show up. This is the time to try out one's inner Brad Pitt, Picasso, or Yo-Yo Ma. This is the time to discover one's hatred for field hockey. This is the time to fall in love with robotics. This is the time to become involved for the sake of fun, curiosity, commitment, and experience, not for the sake of an application.

2. **Take time to teenage.** (Yes, teenage *is* a verb.) Go to prom, learn to drive, fall in love, speak your mind, protest something, fight with Mom, and have a story to tell. (An essay topic needs to start somewhere!) High school may be imperfect and trying and emotional and hard. But if a student didn't allow himself time for activities that didn't "count," he might never discover his true passions.

3. **Don't spend money to build a résumé.** Admissions officers don't expect everyone to fly to Florence with their Italian club. There

---

* Contrary to lots of advice given on the topic, I never once questioned a student who quit an activity, providing he had other interests. But if an applicant quit all activities senior year, it would give me pause.

are enough ways to involve oneself in the community without opening a wallet. Personally, I always preferred to read an application from a student who earned money rather than spent it.

When it comes to extracurriculars, there is no sense trying to game the system. (Learning Swedish for an application is so 2010.) There is no sense in being something that you're not. (Feigning passion for painting is sad.) There's no need to attempt to check every box. (Who really has the time?) Instead I encourage students to recognize what makes their heart beat, what makes them lose track of time, what pulls them out of bed in the morning. A student needs to be doing something, but he doesn't need to be doing everything.

"She doesn't have time for socializing," a counselor (whom I'd known for years) whispered to me after a visit to her high school. "Every day after school, she either captains the debate team, edits the school newspaper, or leads the Diversity Outreach group. Then she heads to the library to perfect her schoolwork until closing." She leaned in with a knowing grin. "She's doing it all."

I looked over at the girl who was sitting at a desk in the college counseling room, studying an SAT prep book. "I'm sure she's very talented."

"I'd love to introduce you, if you have a minute. I know that you aren't going to have time to meet with students individually, but Lily is a special one."

My visit to the school had already run over. I was hungry, cranky, and ready for ketchup-drenched fast food. But my burger would have to wait. "Sure." I shrugged.

I followed the counselor over to the student and was introduced. The student shook my hand with so much vigor, I thought she'd break it. "Very nice to meet you, Ms. Rebecca." She looked at the counselor and whispered, "I thought she wasn't meeting with students."

"I wasn't," I offered. "But there's always time for a quick hello."

"Hello!" she said enthusiastically. "Hello, hello! I loved your presentation!"

"Thank you."

"And the engineering school sounds amazing."

"It is." I responded. "They work hard and play hard at Thayer."

"Well," the counselor interjected, "Lily just works hard. Did I mention she's been nominated to the county's select student association? It's an honor for both her academic work and her activities."

"That's impressive." I laughed. "But I hope you still find some time for fun."

Lily didn't laugh. "Some." She nodded, as if she was afraid to tell me otherwise. She nodded again as if to prove it to herself. "Some."

"I think she's been spending most of her few free hours collecting more volunteer hours," the counselor added.

"How do you volunteer?"

"Library book reshelving, middle school tutoring in history, and community garden planting," she listed robotically.

"Which is your favorite?"

She looked at me like she'd never considered the question. "All," she said. "But I'm hoping to work a few more hours from the blood drive over the break since it will put me in running for the school's most community hours. If I win that award, I'll be the most decorated student in our school's history."

The counselor leaned in to whisper in my left ear. "I told you she was a good one."

I'd met students like this young woman before. Students so fixed on acing the SATs that they forgot how to read for pleasure. Students checking off boxes instead of developing true interests. Students who walked around campus with their faces in notebooks, too busy studying to appreciate the falling snow. There was no time for these students to stop and smell the roses because everyone was trying to grow a winning variety.

"Unless it 'counts,' there's no time," a college advisor said with a laugh (as if he was bragging) over breakfast with colleagues. (I immediately didn't like the man, or the way he wore his own high school ring on his pinkie.) "And if you want to point fingers, you started this mess," he said with a shrug. "The college admissions process is the reason kids don't sleep anymore. You're expecting too much from them."

He was right. And as much as I didn't like his finger jewelry, I appreciated him calling us out on ruining children's fun (unlike Lily's counselor, who seemed to praise the demise of free time). Considering the competition of the pool, students were fighting for an advantage by checking more "elite" extracurricular boxes. In our pool, there seemed to be fewer summer ice cream scoopers and more summer lab rats. * There were fewer stamp collectors but never-ending trophy collectors. There were fewer babysitters and more bronze medalists. (Personally, I was sad to see so many MVPs but so few sportsmanship awards.) There was no time to be a follower or a wanderer or a tinkerer when everyone was elbowing to be the leader.

Meanwhile, admissions officers were trying to make sense of it all. We'd make sure the student was doing *something*, and then look to see if his interests outside of the classroom were mentioned elsewhere in the application. (If a student was student class president and his recommendations never mentioned it, we wondered how much of an impact his leadership had on the community.) We'd look for students who would make the most of resources available on campus. (Why build a soundproof new yoga studio if nobody intends on using it?) We'd seek students who bring various talents outside of the classroom in addition to their

---

* There is no direct question about summer involvements on the Common Application.

intellectual curiosities. And we'd hope to find students worth bragging about in opening remarks at convocation. (I've been to many dean's speeches where they entertainingly list off the incredible talents of the incoming class.) *

I dreaded the extracurricular page. For me, it was the section of the application that was the most mundane and most difficult to decipher for many reasons. Time commitments were challenging to comprehend. (Did anyone sleep during their multiple forty-hour-per-week commitments? Shelley from Cleveland must have a longer week than the rest of us.) Awards-costumed-as-extracurriculars were often ridiculous. ("Best Smile" is a great honor for a student's dentist.) And expectations for various "leadership" positions varied from school to school. (I mentioned I did nothing as NHS president, right?)

The extracurricular review also showcased how ridiculously competitive our students were. If someone was the Kansas tap dancing champion, we probably were also considering the Oregon tap dancing champion. If someone was president of Boys State, another applicant would be president of Girls State. If someone was a tennis captain, another student would be table tennis captain. And if someone was incredibly well rounded, someone else would be the perfect circle. (And no, we didn't have a preference whether someone was well rounded or highly focused, although many folks asked the question.)

As I reviewed ridiculously long résumés decorated with accomplishments, I couldn't help recognizing the immediate effects of the pressures on young people to do it all. If everyone was doing everything, how were we supposed to make sense of any of it? How could we steer the ship back to less of a rat-race experience? How could we create value in activities that didn't "*count*"?

---

* "Welcome Class of 2021. Among you there are twelve of you named Henry, nine of you born on the Fourth of July, and one of you who voices Bingo the Bulldog in the renowned children's series *Pups in Space*."

By the time I left the office, this was a conversation brewing among admissions professionals. This was a topic discussed by mental health professionals as students risked everything for keeping up inside and outside of the classroom. This was top of mind for parents, students, and community members, who kept speaking to me about the pressures of "doing it all." We had to stop the madness.

I may not have an immediate solution. But I do have insight. In competitive admissions, the length of one's résumé wasn't nearly as important as one would believe. Nobody in our office was counting the number of activities on a student's list, or weighting involvements against one another. (Without even keeping track of our talent pool, we were able to pretty much guarantee we'd have enough students to keep our clubs and activities filled.) A student whose flashiest extracurricular was math team could compete with the Kansas tap dancing champion, providing he proved to us that team-solving polynomials was worth a hoot.

For example, consider the following three applicants. Each is summarized in the same way I would record notes on a student's extracurricular engagements. (In many competitive college offices, admissions officers are provided limited space to comment broadly on one's extracurricular profile.)

Adam is Boys State delegate, VP of student council, and lead actor in regional production of *Grease*. Counselor notes theater is a college interest and that he's talented in both musicals and plays.

Bryn is debate president, field hockey co-captain, and is taking self-taught, online Mandarin classes. Latin teacher says she has a knack for quickly learning languages.

Corey is choir secretary, a varsity softball player, and yearbook treasurer. Her counselor notes her impact in changing school social dynamic by solely persuading peers to abolish exclusive class yearbook superlatives and instead allow EACH student to name his own. (Corey has awarded herself "Class Upcycler.")

Although Corey's activities are less traditionally competitive, her engagement with an activity is certainly more memorable. While Adam might partake in a college musical and Bryn might contribute to a language club, Corey's interest in inclusivity might allow her to change the social dynamic of campus in unseen ways. (We'd look for more evidence of this sort of initiative in other parts of the application.)

Admissions officers cared about how extracurriculars complemented one's candidacy. When filling out an application, students are limited in their ability to communicate their interests. But there are ways to strengthen an (authentic) extracurricular section.

1. List extracurricular activities from most important to least important.

The Common Application allows a student to list ten extracurricular involvements. As a reviewer, I expected that the list would be organized by one's most meaningful activities. I also expected that students would use the Honors section on the application to list prizes, awards, and acknowledgments for their passions. (There was no need using space in the extracurricular section for "Social Studies Department Prize" when it could be listed in the Honors section.)

As a side note, some applicants submitted a résumé with their applications. Résumés can be helpful to bring to alumni interviews. But as shameful as it is to admit, I spent very little time looking at folks' résumés during application review. I figured that if something wasn't important enough to list on the extracurricular section of the application, it wasn't worth my time reviewing on a résumé.

2. Don't waste precious space listing every men's gymnastics award.

When admissions officers review activities, they'll summarize one's major achievement in each discipline. There's no need to list all regional, state, and county awards given for men's gymnastics. (A detailed brag sheet is best saved for a coach.) Focus on one's top awards within one discipline (e.g., *Men's Gymnastics: Junior Olympian and Iowa State Champion*) and move on.

3. Nontraditional activities still matter.

Nothing of personal importance is irrelevant. It was relevant to an admissions committee if a student was the neighborhood dog walker, the point person for family finance, or the primary caretaker for younger siblings. (Bonus points for potty training.) Just because an activity isn't sanctioned by a school or community doesn't mean it doesn't matter. (And don't sweat the Common Application extracurricular required drop-down list of "categories." We weren't concerned with the activity category but rather the activity itself.)

4. Be as descriptive as possible.

The Common Application allows approximately 150 character spaces for each activity description. Many applicants keep these descriptions generic, but specificity is much more helpful to an application reviewer. (And no unexplained acronyms, please. Did DCB stand for Drably Costumed Ballerinas? Dutiful Coffee Baristas? District of Columbia Bagpipers?) Application reviewers are less interested in titles and more interested in impact. For example:

> *Unhelpful activity description:* Class Vice President: led senior
>   class in school-wide fundraisers and functions.
> *Helpful activity description:* Class Vice President: created and
>   implemented first school-wide daily e-newsletter. Solely
>   solicited over $1K in newsletter ads, with profits deposited
>   into prom fund.

5. Don't fill boxes to fill boxes.

Empty activity boxes won't prevent a student's college admission. But lackluster energy on the page for one's few activities will. Depth (and enthusiasm) over breadth is essential.

At Dartmouth, we wanted to admit the next John Legend (as confirmed by our music department). But we also needed to admit students who would work the next John Legend's stadium security, design the next John Legend's concert T-shirts, feed the next John Legend's crowds, and buy the next John Legend's music. We needed leaders who could be followers (yes, FOLLOWERS), speakers who could be listeners, critics who could be connectors, presidents who could be faces in the crowd. We needed a little bit of everything and everything in little bits. And we had the freedom to fill these needs within an entire class. We didn't expect (or want) a single student to do it all.

Personally, I longed to know more about how students spent their time in the in-between. I would have loved to read an application from a marching band trumpet player who made time for nightly firefly viewings. Or an art club member who spent her weekends perfecting a chicken tortilla soup recipe. Or a leader of the Black Students Union who built the neighborhood snow fort for the kids on his street. (In 2016, Dartmouth students canceled that year's eighty-year-old tradition of building the Winter Carnival snow sculpture, citing lack of natural snow and lack of student interest. When it happened, I couldn't help but think that students had gotten a little too serious if they weren't willing to play in the snow.) A student's interests didn't have to be school sanctioned, but I hoped they'd be thoughtful. I was interested in young people who still made time for fireflies, for chicken soup, for snowmen.

Extracurricular interests matter because they shape a person, not because they strengthen a résumé. As a reviewer of extracurriculars, I can assure students that there is no magical formula, no perfect activity sequence, no guarantee that any résumé will ensure a student's college admission. Instead, students who are active and engaged outside the classroom will remain competitive in the pool. They'll stand out for the *context* of their extracurriculars, rarely *because* of their extracurriculars. (I say rarely because the Oscar-nominated short film in a foreign language nominee is still going to catch our attention, provided, of course, her application is not otherwise terrible.)

Best of all, students who participate in activities because they're interested might just become more interesting. They might become more curious community members. They might care about something other than résumés. And they might become better *people*, not just better college applicants.

A few months after meeting Lily, the young woman "who didn't have time for socializing," her counselor forwarded me their school newsletter. Lily was featured for being admitted to her top choice competitive school. (She never applied to Dartmouth because according to her counselor she had "enough other safeties.") A photograph accompanied the article, showing Lily holding up her letter, beaming from ear to ear. The headline read, *"School Scholar Scores* Elite College Admission."*

I imagined Lily was thrilled with her outcome. She looked much happier in the photo than she had looked in person. She obviously had checked the right boxes for this college. (I'm confident that any college reading her résumé would have been pleased with her many accomplishments. But I couldn't help but wonder if any part of her application tipped off her extreme intensity.)

As I stared at her picture, I couldn't help but contemplate Lily's future. She might receive a so-called elite diploma. She might get a competitive job offer at the end of her four years. She might continue to build her résumé with elite awards and distinguished honors.

But she'd probably never have time for snow sculptures. She'd likely never stop box checking. She'd assumedly never know the freedom and potential of an unscheduled afternoon. And for that, my heart broke for her.

---

* "Scores" and "wins" are words that made my skin crawl when discussing college admissions.

CHAPTER NINE

TESTING

Even though they had great grades, belonged to clubs, had quirks and interests and passions, students were often described to me only by their standardized testing scores. Parents, coaches, counselors, and students summarized them with a series of digits. It was ludicrous really. But I understood the sentiment.

When I was in high school, my SAT score defined my academic worth. It was a number deemed important by those around me. (To prepare for the test, my parents fed me a "good dinner"* and ensured that I slept enough.)† It was a number that seemed to sum up my "smartness" as compared to other kids applying to college. (I believed I should have scored higher than a ditzy friend who bragged publicly about her score.) It was a number that was perplexing, considering I scored higher on math than verbal (even though math was my weakest and most dreaded subject). And it was a number that stood for both my potential and my achievement.

Years after taking the test, I still remember my exact score (and its verbal and math breakdown). I figured that my husband's score would be as familiar to him. (Sure, we'd talked about the SATs generally, but we'd never talked *numbers*.) "Honey Bunny,‡ what did you score on the

---

* A carb-loaded plate of pasta with meat sauce.

† On one memorable evening, my father complained to the biker's bar next door that their motorcycle-revving clients in the parking lot were keeping his daughter from her needed sleep before the tests.

‡ I used this pet name when I needed my husband to watch the kids, lay off the scented moisturizer, or give me the larger half of the chocolate cruller.

SATs?" I asked as I sat next to him on the couch, sharing popcorn and flipping through television stations.

"I don't remember," Jamal replied.

I nudged him. "Of course, you remember."

"Um." He hesitated. "Maybe in the twelves. Or maybe an eleven something. Actually, I think it was somewhere in the thirteens. I don't really know."

I was sure Jamal knew his number. Everyone knew their numbers. He just didn't want to tell me. To break the ice, I told him my number.

"Really?" he said as he turned to face me.

I was taken aback. "Do you think that's high or low?"

"I mean, neither," he backpedaled as he returned to the television.

I grabbed the remote control and turned it off. "Did you think I'd have a higher number? Do I have a higher score than you? Or is my score lower than you'd expect?"

"I'm just surprised you remember."

My husband remembered his hockey jersey numbers from his peewee program. He remembered how many tomato and mozzarella kabobs he ate the day of our wedding. He remembered every character's first and last name in the *Godfather* trilogy. The fact that standardized test scores weren't important enough to him to remember shocked me.

For the next month, I peppered my girlfriends with questions about their numbers. I didn't need to know their numbers (unless they wanted to share), but I wanted to know if they remembered. Some did remember. Some didn't. Some shared their numbers. Some didn't. But they all had an opinion about testing as an evaluative measure for colleges.

Surprisingly, the friend who scored very well wasn't a believer in test scores as evidence of intellectual potential. "I mean, I did well, but I was good at *testing*," she shrugged. "College was still hard for me."

The friend who didn't perform well was still an advocate for tests. "It may not be perfect, but I'm not sure how else we could measure a student's aptitude at a particular moment in time."

The longer I worked in admissions, the more I fell somewhere in the middle of the testing debate. For an application reviewer, testing was a helpful data point when considering thousands of applications. But I wasn't as convinced (as I was in high school) that a test score was worth obsessing about (or remembering for twenty years). I'd met too many testers on both sides of the testing spectrum to feel strongly about testing as a predictive evaluator of a student's success in college.

Plus, research had proved that a student's score was contextual. Studies concluded that the number one prediction of how students scored on tests was based on their income level. In addition, national standardized testing averages differed depending on a student's race. (One of the more referenced studies on this topic is 2013's "Race, Poverty and SAT Scores," written by UPenn researcher Ezekiel J. Dixon-Román, USC researcher John J. McArdle, and City University of New York researcher Howard T. Everson. This study publishes details about the correlation between a family's income, race, and standardized test scores. In their research, they found that wealthy students scored higher on the SATs compared to their low-income peers. When race was considered, the difference in SAT scores between socioeconomic classes was twice as large among Black students compared to white students.) Scores were imperfect, flawed, and often misleading about a student's potential. And yet we as a nation continued to lead conversations about our children with their scores.

"She's a thirty-six,"* the mother bragged.

I was standing on a sidewalk in Hanover, speaking to an acquaintance I'd only ever seen at the gym. "That's terrific!" I smiled. "Where's she headed?"

"Stanford," the mother answered. "But it wasn't her first choice. She

---

* A 36 is a perfect score on the ACT.

really wanted Princeton. It's amazing that a perfect ACT couldn't get her into Princeton. I mean those kids must have found a way to score thirty-sevens."

I couldn't remember the name of her daughter. I couldn't remember if she had attended our local public high school. I didn't know a gosh darn thing about the student except that she received a perfect score on the ACT. And in this case, that was all the mother felt the need to mention. "It's competitive, surely." I shrugged.

"We were just thrilled with her score." She shook her head. "I couldn't be prouder."

I knew that the mother was proud of the daughter and not just the score. But in this case, in my case, and in many other cases, we were considering testing as a piece of one's identity. Applicants and families sometimes spoke of the numbers as if they were part of a student's DNA.

Standardized testing is one of the most discussed topics in college admissions. It's cheered and jeered as one of the most controversial pieces of a college application. It's misunderstood by many, overestimated by some, and underestimated by few.

The Dartmouth Admissions Office knew our standardized testing profile was very much in the public eye. We talked about testing frequently, discussing both the good and the bad. Every November, during our annual admissions reading kickoff retreat, rookie and veteran readers would spend significant time considering the use of testing in an applicant's review. We'd discuss the implications of socioeconomic status and race/ethnicity on one's score. We'd learn and relearn our own system for recording testing as a data point in the application. We'd argue (among ourselves) the fairness, importance, and equity of standardized testing in application review.

Yet we, and many other colleges, knew test results were not only helpful in providing standardization in an otherwise nonstandard process, but they also boosted a college's prestige. (Test-optional schools typically only report the scores students report, thereby helping their test averages as well.) Dartmouth, like every other school, wanted to be coveted. The stronger a university's average test scores, the more coveted the university. The more coveted the university, the stronger the applicant's standardized test scores. It was a never-ending cycle dependent on growth in numbers.

College officials know testing is flawed. But in addition to providing a standardized data point for admissions review, higher scores help preserve a college's academic reputation. Admissions offices know that putting too much emphasis on testing will surely socially backfire. (No college wants applicants to feel like monumental testing is a prerequisite for admission.) But many colleges aren't prepared to abandon testing altogether. Dartmouth, like so many other institutions, softened our testing policies to be friendly to test takers (while still requiring the exams).

- **We reviewed an applicant's score "in context" of a complete application.**

A holistic approach to admissions review meant testing was one data point of many. A score's significance fluctuated based on an individual's background, perspective, and academic resources. The greater distance traveled to college access, the more lenient colleges often were with scores.

- **We accepted late scores.**

If a student first submitted an application to the college, we'd happily wait for "late" testing, providing we'd receive the scores with time to make final decisions. (In other words, we'd still accept November test date scores for early decision applications, even though the deadline to apply was November 1. We'd also accept February scores for regular decision applications, even though the deadline to apply was January 1.)

- **We (happily) "superscored" test results.**

A "superscore" is the marriage of a student's highest individual test scores from different test sections on different dates. (If a student scored a 500 Verbal, 600 Math on the October SAT, then scored a 600 Verbal and a 500 Math on the November SAT, we'd count the 600 Verbal from November and the 600 Math from October.) Superscoring strengthened our own class averages while also helping each student. Individual colleges have various subpolicies on superscoring. (For example, Dartmouth superscored the SAT, not the ACT. But if a student took both the ACT and the SAT, we'd compare the scores and use the highest equivalent.) I suggest that students check for testing policies to fully understand how their scores will be reviewed.

We wanted to make testing as easy as possible, knowing it was a hurdle for most students. (We regularly reminded students to request testing fee waivers from their counselors.) We knew we were at fault for creating a frenzy around these tests. (Few students were as obsessed with their midterm literature exam as they were with their verbal SAT.) And we knew that in order to recruit a class of diverse talents, we'd have to downplay the role of testing in application review in conversations with prospective students.

"I just don't think my testing represents me," Mandy said during our meeting in a conference room in Little Rock.

"Me neither," Jodi chimed in. "Testing is useless. Nobody does well on those tests, and if they do, they don't have a life outside of studying."

I'd heard the argument against testing many times from students. I was well equipped to appease their concerns. "Look, I'm not saying you need a perfect test score to get in . . ."

"But you're showing us pamphlets where the averages are above what we have," Jodi announced.

She was right. We printed the numbers right on our brochures as if they were nutritional guidelines for the college. "These are *averages*," I said as I pointed to the numbers. "That means half of the population on campus has scores lower than this number."

As the words left my mouth, I felt like a creep. As much as college admissions officers would play up our rankings, we'd publicly downplay our average SAT scores in recruiting efforts. (After all, we're *professional* recruiters.) We'd breeze through averages in conversation. We'd pretend the numbers didn't really matter.

"So you're saying that if I have an 1110, I have a chance of going to Dartmouth."

"Everyone has a *chance*," I responded.

"Well, then do I have a good chance?"

"*Nobody* has a good chance."

"Well, then why is it worth applying, even if students with perfect scores don't have a good chance?"

I took a deep breath. It was a good question. My job was to encourage everyone to apply to Dartmouth. My job was to make sure students knew that we cared for more than standardized testing. But my job was not to mislead students into believing admission into college without strong scores will be easy.

"You should apply because you shouldn't let your scores dictate an otherwise exceptional application."

I didn't know if Mandy's and Jodi's applications would be exceptional. But I did know that their circumstances placed them in an exceptional subsection of our application pool. These young women attended a community-based organization in Little Rock that helped underserved students find college support. The students at this CBO were mostly minority students from low-income families, all of whom qualified for testing fee waivers. They had been identified in their community as bright young people with top academic credentials, but they didn't have the schooling and support history of other applicants in the pool. We didn't expect their scores to be equivalent to the scores of students with SAT tutors. But we did expect their transcripts to be.

Jodi nodded as she considered my words. "Mandy's pretty darn smart." She tilted her head toward her friend. "She's definitely Dartmouth material."

"So are you, Jodi." Mandy nodded back. "Mr. Tilton said you're the best student in the district."

The girls traded compliments for a minute or so. It was lovely to see them build themselves up, without allowing the scores to rip each other down. And when they remembered I was still sitting there, Mandy turned to me. "So, I guess we should ask you about your chemistry major. I mean, since we're Dartmouth material and all."

In my career, I didn't want any prospective student to feel as though their low standardized test scores prohibited them from being admitted to a college. But the truth was that at Dartmouth their low scores would have to be accompanied by an incredibly strong application in other ways. It would be difficult to admit a student with low scores without arguing his case *despite his scores*. (Back in the days of paper files, an unnamed rookie colleague would pick through files, choosing those with low test scores, hoping they'd be quicker reads. He'd learn that applications to Dartmouth with low test scores were never quicker reads. They were always more complicated, more layered, and often more compelling.)

Savvy students generally know if their applications will be competitive in a university's pool (even if they don't know if they'll be admitted). Most seem self-aware enough to know if their academic credentials qualify their applications for being contenders. (Even if I had received a perfect score on the SAT, I didn't belong in the MIT pool. I wasn't strong enough academically in my own high school, never mind on a national scale.) At Dartmouth, we didn't have a lot of students apply who didn't belong in the pool. (Again, it was a self-selecting process.) But there were students who didn't apply because they didn't know that they *did* belong in the pool.

I pushed students with top-level academic backgrounds to apply to Dartmouth even if their scores were below the norm. This included rich students, poor students, students of color, white students, and everyone in between. An under-resourced Black student from California might have weak scores but the strongest GPA in his high school's long history. A wealthy Asian American student from North Carolina might have below-average scores but the strongest recommendations (in terms of tangible and intangible qualities) I'd read all year. I didn't want to discourage or encourage students *because* of their testing, but rather because of their other academic talents. A college's average testing was a useful reference point, but it certainly wasn't the rule.

After years of working in competitive college admissions, I learned that testing mattered. Exceptional testing certainly helped a strong student. But testing wasn't *everything*. We knew that students of certain socioeconomic levels were at an advantage when testing. We also knew that testing didn't represent a student's daily efforts in a classroom. When all other qualifications were equal, most admissions officers I knew would rather take a valedictorian with slightly-below-our-average testing scores than an average student with perfect scores. (Either way, a college's academic profile would be boosted, either by students in the reported "top decile of their class" or by testing.) And we didn't sweat minor differences in scores. (In my perspective, one student's 660 Verbal was as good as another student's 670. Splitting hairs about similar scores seemed ridiculous.)

Of course, perfect test takers didn't want to believe me when I told them that they couldn't rest on their laurels. (There are lots of arguments to admit smart kids who are poor test takers. But there isn't a lot of sympathy for strong test takers who aren't performing in the daily classroom.) A high math SAT score only meant we'd expect to see an

A in calculus. A five on the AP Biology exam meant we'd better see a superlative recommendation from an AP Biology teacher. (We'd expect more than "academics come easy" from a teacher recommendation for a high scorer.) A perfect TOEFL* meant we'd expect perfect English grammar on the essay.

And imperfect test takers wouldn't believe me when I'd tell them they had a shot, providing other parts of their applications were exceptional. (Again, I never wanted a student to think that less-than-average test scores canceled out an otherwise compelling application.) While it was harder to be admitted with weaker testing, it certainly wasn't impossible.

The truth is that better testing could only help a student's admissions probability. Today, I advise students to optimize their test-taking support. (A quick google search can help a student find plenty of online tools to help prepare.) I recommend that they complete testing requirements as early as possible, allowing time for retesting if necessary. (I recommend prospective students first take their SAT during their junior spring or the summer before senior year. By senior fall, a student will likely want to retest.) And I urge students to stop worrying about how it looks to an admissions committee if they test once, twice, or twelve times. (Since our processing folks superscored the test results, it didn't matter, nor did I personally ever care.)

Furthermore, applicants should be aware of how "additional testing" can round out their testing profiles. In addition to the SAT or ACT, many colleges recommend, require, or accept further exam results to prove a student's competency. A student should check for college-specific policies. Other testing, such as AP scores and state/regional testing, may be relevant in some cases.

_____

* The TOEFL test (or Test of English as a Foreign Language) was one testing option for students who attended schools where the language of primary instruction was not English. These (predominantly international) students could prove their English proficiency by completing this or other English language exams.

• **AP Scores**

Not every student can and should take Advanced Placement courses at his school. (Schools like my local Hanover High School don't offer APs.) But for students in Advanced Placement tracks, taking the concluding AP test could help one's application AND eventual college credit.

Most colleges will consider AP test scores, if submitted. It seems that most of these schools have optional policies toward AP reporting, so students can select to submit only their strongest AP scores. (Although occasionally, schools will report all AP scores on transcripts, so students might want to check their school policies.) Some colleges will also use these results for first-year college placement (or credit) in courses. (For example, if a student scores a 4 on their AP French exam, they qualify to "jump" a level in college French.)

As a word of caution, however, I was always wary of the student who submitted *multiple* AP self-study exam scores without taking the classes. (Personally, I'd care more about a student's grade in an AP class than his score on the final test.) I understand why a student might want to self-study AP material, but taking many AP tests without having taken AP classes felt disingenuous if one had other academic options.

• **State/Regional Testing**

Occasionally, state/regional exam scores were printed on high school transcripts. While admissions officers don't focus on these tests, anything submitted with an application was fair game for review. (The New York State Regents Examination was a regular offender, often published on New York high school transcripts.) While we recognized that state tests varied in length and substance, we occasionally commented on a student's results if his scores were (either positively or negatively) noteworthy.

Regardless of which specific tests are submitted, students can always be their own testing advocates. It's smart to comment on (not whine about) one's own testing if there's something relevant to say. (Commentary can be provided in the "Additional Information" section or on its own in an e-mail to a regional officer.) For example:

I had the flu during the October SAT but have reregistered for the November testing date.

I took the AP German Language exam on my own because my school cut our German program after my second year of instruction. I self-studied for two more years and am proud of my 4 score.

A lice infestation at the ACT hosting school caused testing delays and itchy scalps.

Helpful insight was always welcome, particularly in the case of lower-than-average scores.

No perfect score has an admissions guarantee. No imperfect score has a denial guarantee. And while testing can help a student arrive at the gate, rarely does it solely push a student through the gate. While folks are obsessing, remembering, forgetting, and dismissing their standardized test scores, the one thing I know for sure is that a person is more than her number.

"I'm a 3.8 and a 1280," the young woman said to me at a New York City college fair. "What chance do I have?"

I received this sort of question from prospective students often. And I couldn't answer their questions. Perhaps this student's 3.8 GPA was calculated on a 6.0 scale. Perhaps her verbal SAT was a 480 and her math was an 800. Perhaps her junior-year curriculum included six periods of study hall. Perhaps she was a first-generation college student from a low-income family at an under-resourced public school with no honors curriculum. No number would help me estimate her admissions fate.

"Let's start with our names." I extended my hand and shook hers. "My name is Becky."

"I'm Sarah," the young woman responded.

Now we were getting somewhere.

CHAPTER TEN

THE PERSONAL STATEMENT

After the recommendations have been requested, after the testing has been completed, after one has purchased a blue and orange *Go Hornets* mug at the Kalamazoo bookstore, it's time to sit down with one's thoughts. It's time to consider one's biggest "challenge, setback, or failure." (Alas, the ol' personal failure question is usually one of the many Common Application prompts.) It's time to remember the correct usage of "its" and "it's." And then *it's* time to start writing the personal statement.

The number one secret to writing a great personal statement is, at the risk of being obvious, to keep it personal and make a statement. It's not about shock. It's not about a fancy vocabulary. It's not about any magic formula. (Although I've heard the joke that if a student mentions beloved alumnus Arthur Ashe three times in a UCLA essay, he's automatically admitted.) It's a human narrative with a point.

I've read about twenty-six thousand essays in my career. When folks ask me about my favorite essays, I should have many from which to choose. The truth is that I only remember about a dozen.

I remember the essay from the young man who raised snakes. (I have a fear of serpents, and while his essay was incredibly well done, my skin crawled with his every word.) I remember the "Class Clown" who defended the relevance of his title in the classroom. (He convinced me that we need more humor in education.) And I remember "The Sweaty Zoo Greeter." (More on this later.) But I don't remember the majority of the others.

Most essays weren't memorable because most essays were good. Really good. The personal statements served their purpose by saying something about the applicant and giving context to the application. They might not have stood out to an admissions director who read twenty essays daily. (Seriously, how many *Jeopardy!* questions can one recall after watching hundreds of episodes?) But they were exactly what they should have been.

I tell this to students not to depress them about their own chances of writing a memorable essay, but instead to give them relief against having to write The Great American College Essay. No one essay made me stand up and clap. No one essay was *ever* going to make me stand up and clap. Instead, the essays would make me smile, think, or understand a person's point of view. The purpose of an essay was to share a story, a vision, a thought. The purpose of an essay was never to win an award.

Of course, finding the right 650 words* can be brutal. And students regularly admit they feel pressure to write on substantial topics. The pressures to write The Great American College Essay are plenty, and the prompts are vague enough to allow for topic paralysis. (Personally, I wished they eliminated the "Topic of Choice" because it is too open-ended. We didn't need essays on burger preferences to qualify.)

I'm sympathetic to how hard it is to write a college essay. I've been asked many times for advice. There's already a lot of decent advice out there. ("*Write something you'd want to read.*" "*Spellcheck, edit, spellcheck again.*" "*Write an essay, not a research paper.*") But after reading thousands of personal statements, I have my own suggestions.

1. Be specific.

Admissions officers don't need a summary of one's entire summer. Instead, a simple moment can capture the energy and experience. For example:

OKAY TOPIC: *I enjoyed practicing my Spanish language during a family trip to Barcelona.*

---

* There is a limit of 650 words for the personal statement on the Common Application.

BETTER TOPIC: *I learned the importance of mastering a foreign language when I ordered "orange milk" instead of "orange juice" at a Spanish restaurant.*

2. **Don't write an essay about your grandmother, your soccer coach, or Hermione Granger.**

The "My Grandmother Is My Hero" essay makes an admissions officer want to admit the applicant's grandmother. Same goes for the essay about the soccer coach. And Hermione had her moment. Better topics are:

"The Summer I Taught Grandma How to Use Chopsticks"
"The Art of Refereeing Toddler Soccer"
"My Summer as the Lowville Library Book Recommender"

Students need to remember that the essay needs to be about themselves. While Hermione might have inspired generations, she inspired *generations*. The essay isn't going to be original if millions of young people could write the same essay. (Nobody wants to read about Taylor Swift, deceased pets, or the war against plastic straws, either.) Which brings me to . . .

3. **Write an essay only you can write.**

In essay-writing presentations (which were rare), I led students in the following exercise.

Imagine all the essays from your school have been taped to a wall. Names have been removed from the essays. Now imagine your best friend enters the room and reads every essay. Would she identify your essay? What if she had to find your essay in a room filled with all the essays from the county? From the state? From the country?

An essay about winning a school debate tournament isn't specific enough. An essay about being nervous before a school debate tournament isn't specific enough. But an essay about using one's debate skills to single-handedly challenge the superintendent to allow a local Vietnamese food truck driver to park (and serve) on school grounds might just make the grade.

The topic doesn't have to be lofty. In the case above, the debating student had quite a story to tell. But I've read essays about much simpler topics. "Realizations from Changing My Daily Morning Seat on the A-Train" works just as well.

4. Make sure your main point is an admissions officer's main takeaway.

Behind the scenes, admissions officers summarize essays for committee members who don't have time to read them. When I read essays, I'd summarize with a sentence, followed by an overall single-word judgment. For example:

Juan spends free time at animal shelter and is passionate about local spaying/neuter programs. Good.

Maverick's broken leg taught him patience during football season. Okay.

Abbie produces her own at-home cooking show (with one thousand web subscribers) specializing in soups. Well done.

An "okay" essay wouldn't be the kiss of death. A "well done" essay wouldn't be enough to solely move an application to admit. Instead, the personal statement would complement the rest of the application. (*Her soup essay proves that Abbie is more versatile than just a computer science whiz.*)

It's good practice for students to summarize their essay in a single sentence. It's useful to imagine what an admissions officer would take away from one's words. If an essay seems to be missing the point, I'd encourage a rewrite.

Essays were expected to be written by high school students, not Pulitzer Prize winners. There was no need to use words we'd both need to look up in the dictionary. (Some students committed *circumlocution* just by using the word.) There was no need to insert adjectives just to creep up to the word-count limit. (I never counted words, but I would wager most students wrote 649 words for their essay.) There was no need to choose lofty topics and ambitious ideas. (*"Before I begin, I'd like to discuss the security crisis in Burundi."*)

Still, some students can't help but throw a little glitter on the glue of their personal statements. I know a lot about glitter-throwing firsthand. (I often believed we should have renamed the personal statement the "overstatement.") After graduate school and before working full-time at Dartmouth, I took a position at a two-week camp for college-bound seniors to help them craft their essays. (The word "craft" being incredibly apropos considering many of them were desperate to create something out of very little.) I tried to help students make their essays more dramatic, more comedic, more thoughtful. I encouraged them to rethink "What I Learned About Poor People on My Expensive Family Vacation to Honduras" and instead write "How Honduran Cuisine Inspired My Home Cooking." I helped them deliver a powerful opening sentence. I workshopped their essay with peers. And I hoped to send them home from camp with an admissions-ready, perfectly worded, 649-word personal statement.

I never wrote a word of their essays. I never put words in their mouth. But I sure encouraged some ideas over others. "Crafting" essays often felt like debate practice. Convincing youngsters to change their topics was difficult. And at the end of the day, it felt crummy assisting these students while I knew others (with fewer resources) struggled with the same assignment.

I know many students seek professional help. And from my experience meeting these professionals at conferences, I've learned that they run the gamut in terms of helpfulness, price, and ethics. The 2019 "Varsity Blues" scandal aside (which was a criminal admissions bribery investigation of college consultant Rick Singer and his many high-powered clients, including actresses Lori Loughlin and Felicity Huffman), I met a few independent counselors whose "assistance" was difficult to gauge. At the same time, I met many other independent counselors who seemed ethical and well intentioned. (Like any career, there are the duds, the studs, and the regular ol' Janes and Joes trying to make a living.) And even students without professional help can find free advice and guidance through nonprofit organizations and various websites. (Of course, the playing field is uneven for some students with little college admissions support. At Dartmouth, we tried to give essay workshops for students from under-resourced communities during our various "Fly-In"events.)

Both the most curated essay and the rawest personal statement (spell-checked, of course) likely still wouldn't be memorable to a seasoned admissions officer. In the moment, I'd cry at a young man's account of leaving his family in a war-torn country to pursue education. I'd connect with a student's experience conquering the mile run in gym class. I'd admire a student's work to diversify hotel hair care products for people of color. But then I'd move on to the next application. I'd read the next student's words on a page. I'd forget about hair care products and be introduced to one's love of Chinese checkers.

In high school, I made the mistake of thinking that I could write The Great American College Essay and earn admission through my words. After hemming and hawing on topics, I finally wrote about my experience with refugees from Cuba. (While offshore fishing, my family had assisted men in inner tubes who were fighting for their lives.) I wrote about the Cuban men's sacrifice and courage as they sat days in the Atlantic Ocean, drifting and dehydrated. It was an incredible experience for me as a middle schooler. But the refugees were the heroes of this story. My essay said little about *me*.

I, like many other college applicants, felt the pressure to write something substantial. My experience with refugees from Cuba was substantial. My counselor told me to write the refugee story. My parents and English teacher agreed. And so, I did. I wrote with passion about the men who braved the Atlantic for freedom. Their story was important. My story was . . . fine. It likely didn't get me admitted to colleges. It likely didn't get me denied.

When I wrote my essay, I didn't have the perspective of the thousands of other essays being written by college-bound young people. I didn't know that it would have been more personal, and thus more memorable to an admissions officer, if I had written about how my loss in a local jingle competition inspired me to become a better writer. (I still mourn the loss of first prize, a backyard garden sculpture, which my ninth-grade self so desperately wanted.) I didn't know that admissions officers weren't looking for "substantial" topics but heartfelt ones. And I certainly didn't know that essays mostly confirmed candidacies rather than catapulted them.

Of course, there was one essay I read in my career that hit all the right notes. It wasn't written by a person who protested his government or won Nassau County Singing Idol or had a talent for speaking pig Latin. It was simpler. It was accessible. It was entertaining. (To protect confidentiality, I'm going to change some identifiable details of the essay, but believe me, it was just as good.)

Laurie was a young woman who had always been fascinated by animal biology. After applying to (and being accepted at) a competitive zoo internship, she showed up ready to learn about the behavior of lions, tigers, and bears. She shared her interest in zoology and her hope to someday work in wildlife preservation at the beginning of her statement. But with an overenrolled intern program and an understaffed zoo, the managers needed to fill a vacancy in the park "greeter" program. While the other interns were placed with zoologists, Laurie was chosen to stand at the entrance of the park (come rain, shine, or humidity) and offer exhibit directions to confused guests. In her essay, she explained that the most popular question was simply about how to locate the nearest restroom.

I loved this statement for many reasons. It proved Laurie's interest in zoology and her initiative in applying to the zoo intern program. It showed her ability to take on a less-than-thrilling task. (I knew Laurie would be the type of kid who wouldn't complain if given a dishwashing position as an on-campus job.) It showed a sense of humor and decency. ("Most people wanted to see the pandas first. But I found myself cheering for the sole person who asked to see the prairie dogs.") And it highlighted her commitment to sticking with something less prestigious than she had hoped. (I knew she was the type of person who wouldn't quit the soccer team if she only made JV.)

Of course, Laurie's story was her own. Other applicants need to consider their stories, their quirks, their motivations, their habits. Then they need to give themselves a break. The admissions process isn't meant to be an essay contest. Shakespeare himself might have bored an admissions committee with an essay on Macbeth. But personal statements can add a little spunk, a little spice, a little character to an otherwise straightforward admissions process.

Yes, some essays are coached, and some essays are highly edited. But the best essays are sometimes just the good essays. They don't have to be works of art. They don't have to be the most memorable writing sample. They just have to say something of personal interest.

And we all have something to say.

CHAPTER ELEVEN

SUPPLEMENTAL ESSAYS

In addition to the personal statement, many colleges require "supplemental essays" from their applicants. As a reader, I found that while personal statements were typically well edited, supplemental essays often felt rushed, half answered, or poorly written. In fact, a college's supplement was often more helpful to me than a personal statement because it read more authentically. (This was a secret of admissions among many of my peers.)

Each individual institution decides what kind of supplemental questions to ask its candidates. Some schools might ask for one short answer (around 200 words) to a specific question. Other schools might require many paragraph-long responses to multiple questions. Still other schools might welcome various other written (and multimedia) submissions.

Of course, some students didn't want to write more than one personal statement. (The point of the Common Application was to streamline the application process, after all.) Some students figured that nothing mattered as much as the essay. I heard many complaints from prospective students and their families.

"The supplements are killing him," the mother said over coffee. "Honestly, he might not apply to his last school because they require three extra short answers."

"Do they really care what my favorite color is?" the young man asked me. "And isn't everyone going to just say that they love orange and blue, the college's official colors?"

"Seriously, why does the college bother to ask about my biggest weakness?" the young woman asked. "Isn't it just a trick question anyway?"

I didn't apologize for making a student write a few extra words. I recognized that students were overburdened with college requirements, but the supplements gave students another opportunity to share details other than grades or scores. (Although I wish we asked questions with more character-confirming answers. *"Do you know the name of your next-door neighbor?" "What town does your school bus driver call home?" "When was the last time you used a postage stamp?"*) I looked forward to reviewing the Dartmouth supplement as I toiled over application pages. And I tried to remind students to pay it some respect.

After all, many colleges ask applicants on the supplement to elaborate on an activity of significance. This is a fabulous opportunity to enhance one's extracurricular profile with a specific example. In my experience, many students used vague, unhelpful language to expand on their favorite involvement. (*"Soccer teaches me teamwork."*) But with some thoughtfulness, an applicant could use this space to hit home a point. As an imagined example:

Most people practice art to express themselves. I do it for the money. I've never considered myself an artist. But when my brother needed an album cover for his rock band, I offered to help. I've always been a doodler. It was never anything I took seriously, but rather a way to keep my hands busy on long bus rides. After my brother's album was released, friends commented on the cover. Soon, I was drawing for the school yearbook, the town newspaper, and the local dentist's office. (They needed a drawing of "Mr. Tooth" for their holiday card.) Drawing taught me how to run a business. I learned how to price my work, how to handle customers' needs, and how to deliver on schedule. I may never be Picasso, but with every drawing, my art becomes better and I collect more entrepreneurial experience. I call that a win.

In addition to the activity elaboration, colleges often asked specific questions of their choosing. Some questions were outrageous. Some were thought-provoking. And some were self-serving. While most colleges had some sort of "Why College X" question, many asked additional questions that fell into the following categories.

Something about you: What is something you have recently changed your mind about and why? (Brandeis)

Something about them: As part of our "Voices of Our Time" series—which allows students, faculty, and staff to hear from some of the world's leading thinkers—Wake Forest has hosted Ta-Nehisi Coates, Michelle Alexander, Eboo Patel, and Thomas Friedman. If you could choose the next series speaker, whom would you pick, and why? (Wake Forest)

Something to break the ice: Name three songs from your perfect playlist. (Elon)

In the answers to these types of questions, application reviewers were looking for specificity. It didn't matter if a student chose his deli butcher, his vice principal, or Will Smith to be Wake Forest's next series speaker, providing he could pointedly defend his choice.

In addition to receiving more personal information on an applicant in her own words, these supplements were good marketing tools for an institution. A college could remind an applicant of its strengths. (*As a university with one of the strongest computer science departments in the country, we would like you to speak to your vision of the future of tech.*) They could use the supplemental questions to make the process feel more personal. (Admissions officers likely didn't care if Stevie Wonder or Stevie Nicks made your ideal playlist, but this question surely was more exciting than asking about an intended major.) And they could add a tinge of humanity to the process.

Supplements simply strengthened one's application (if one took the time to answer questions thoughtfully). Admissions officers wanted to know that students did their homework on their institutions (which again is reason to head "off the beaten path" on campus tours). They wanted to allow a student another opportunity (besides the essay) to share his voice. And they wanted to identify students who were serious enough about a school to write a few extra sentences on an application. (While colleges wanted as many applications as possible, we wanted to admit students who would accept our offers. Why waste admission on a student whose supplement was poorly executed?)

It's important to write a strong personal statement. But it's equally important to spend time on one's supplemental answers. As an admissions officer, I saw too many applications with sloppy supplements and "perfect" applications. Yet the supplement is a chance to expand one's candidacy, to reveal one's personality, and to prove one's interest.

If the essay was the heart of an application, the supplement was its soul. The savviest applicants knew to capitalize on this opportunity. They knew to share specific details to reveal their personalities. And they knew to write a heck of a short answer about their perfect playlist, regardless of their musical choices.

CHAPTER TWELVE

SUBMITTING THE APPLICATION

Colleges are going to admit the students that they need in a class. One spelling error is not going to change an admissions officer's decision. A dazzling vocabulary isn't going to nudge an application into the admit bin. Decisions are based on the whole of each candidacy, the depth of the pool, and the desires of the institution.

But if a student wants his best shot at admission, he needs to care about the application as much as he cares about the college. He needs to pay attention to both the little things and the big things. He needs to carve out time, save his work, and familiarize himself with the application submission software. But most of all, he needs to capitalize on every entry.

As an admissions director, I read approximately 130 applications per week at Dartmouth. That's 240 short answer questions, 360 recommendation letters, and 78,000 essay words weekly. I didn't read a single other thing (including my beloved Sunday *New York Times* newspaper or monthly *Martha Stewart Living* magazine) during reading season. I focused only on the Common Application. And boy, did we grow close.

There are essentially ten sections of a college application. Five sections are completed by the student:

1. Personal details (including demographic, family, and schooling information)
2. Extracurriculars/Honors
3. The Personal Statement
4. Supplemental Essays
5. (Optional) Arts Supplement

The other five sections are submitted by second parties:

6. Testing
7. School Transcript/High School Profile
8. Counselor Recommendation
9. Teacher Recommendations
10. (Optional) Alumni Interview Report

On average, I would spend about twelve minutes reviewing each complete Common Application. Although this number always shocked people, the reading never felt rushed.* Instead, being an experienced reader, I knew which pages I could skim. (A school's fax number wasn't going to change my decision.) I knew which sections needed careful attention. (The reported rank was sometimes forced into deciles.) I knew which areas would throw me for a curve. (Those rare disciplinary action explanations sometimes took a second read. *Was the student suspended for plagiarism in English literature class or for lying about it?*) And I knew where to expect the expected. (*Another Hermione essay, eh?*)

Students (hopefully) were spending more than twelve minutes on their applications. We knew the process was intimidating. We knew it was a hurdle for those without guidance or support. We knew it could be technically challenging. But it was important to fill out these forms carefully. After all, we reviewed applications, not people.

When speaking to students about filling out their college applications, I have two critical pieces of advice.

1. Strategize one's (holistic) attack.

Writing a college application is much like putting together a puzzle. A student needs to start with the corner pieces (testing, transcript, essay,

---

* Thanks to an elementary school reading contest that rewarded students for quickly finishing their copies of The Baby-Sitters Club books, I'd always been a fast reader.

activities) and work one's way inward. A student needs to visualize the big picture. And a student needs focused time (and eyeglasses).

Mostly, students need to consider how to best showcase their strengths in the various parts of the application.

> If a college's supplemental question was going to ask a student about environmentalism, it didn't make sense to write a personal statement on the same topic.

> If a student was going to list cello as a top activity, he should probably submit a music talent supplement.

> If a student wanted to major in French but submitted chemistry and English teacher recommendations, he might want to highlight his leadership in French Club on the supplement.

Applicants needed to consider the big picture in the same way that a reviewer would. It helped to take a step back and to imagine the big take-aways. It was important to plan how to best incorporate one's strengths throughout the holistic application. And it was paramount to consider the application as a whole, not in sections.

2. Be as descriptive as possible.

I often argue that being a college application reviewer is much like being a lawyer: the more evidence available, the stronger the case. A strong application presents the reader with specific answers to *all* relevant questions. A student should carefully submit all "optional" materials. (It irked me when students didn't submit the peer recommendation to Dartmouth.) A student should complete an arts supplement if she has a special talent. (She should not submit a talent supplement if she is not well practiced. A rookie painter's weak art talent rating could hurt an application if she wants to major in art.) And a student should fill every blank space.

Specifically, it's in the best interest of a student to fill out the Common

Application's "Additional Information" section. This section asks applicants to "provide details on circumstances or qualifications not reflected in the application." Most students don't complete this section, likely because they're not sure what to say. But this is an opportunity to speak about one's school experience, family background, culture, or personal story. For example,

A student could tell us about her experience coming out in a conservative high school.

A student could tell us about a peanut allergy limiting his restaurant employment experience.

A student could tell us about being a first-generation college student and wanting to set an example for younger stepsiblings.

Or a student could tell us about meeting Becky, the most amazing admissions officer during a recent trip to campus. (Admissions folks love an ego stroke.)

Students could tell us anything. ANYTHING! Yet I found that many didn't write a single word in this section.

Every student applying to Dartmouth completed the same paperwork. But some applications were more multifaceted. Some were more "complete" than others. (There's no such thing as an "optional" supplement, folks.) Some were richer with details. And some gave us more evidence to "admit."

In my experience, the students who capitalized on the most "minor" things made their applications more dynamic.

1. Sometimes the way a student filled out his family information (*Mother's Occupation: Supermarket Clerk and Personal Hero*) spoke more about his character than his recommendations.

2. Sometimes the way a student explained her activities showed her priorities. (*Senior Class Treasurer: putting my bias aside to creatively budget senior car wash dollars for best prom deejay, even though I'd personally like the money to go to our organic garden.*)

3. Sometimes the way a student inputted basic information showed attention to detail. (I wish I had a dollar for every intended *psychology* major who misspelled the word.)

One applicant was often on my mind when I talked to students about the importance of application details. This young man wrote a heartfelt personal statement. He had one of the top grade point averages in his class. And his recommenders *raved* about his independent science research. Yet his e-mail address was ibrakeforhotmoms@gmail.com. *

When I read Hot Mom's application, I wasn't sure what to do with it. On one hand, I wanted to give him a pass. An e-mail address was such a trivial detail. Chances are he'd been using the same e-mail address since middle school.

On the other hand, the student's e-mail address was speaking to his character. There were plenty of other students chomping at the bit for his seat. And the fact that he, as a seventeen-year-old high school senior, sat down and typed this e-mail address into his college application made me question his choices. (Honestly, I wondered if he purposely sabotaged his application to rebel against college-pushing parents.) His carelessness for his e-mail address spoke volumes.

After some hemming and hawing, I ultimately voted to deny Hot Mom's application. I figured that if a student identified on his college

---

* I've changed his e-mail handle to protect his identity, but I can assure the reader that his actual e-mail address was far worse.

application with such a tag, he was telling us something about himself. While we didn't say that e-mail addresses mattered to an applicant's decision, it was clear that even such a trivial detail could be impactful.

I tell Hot Mom's story to anyone who will listen. It's an extreme example of what happens when an applicant doesn't consider the details. Something as seemingly insignificant as an e-mail address can be an opportunity to say something about oneself. (A prospective student whose e-mail address is letsdriveelectriccars@gmail.com could sneak in one more detail about her interests than another student using firstname-lastname@gmail.com.) Something as seemingly trivial as the "family information section" can help to confirm one student's first-generation status or another student's legacy connections. Something as mundane as listing one's school contact information can show a care for details. (Although I wasn't going to vote to deny a student because he didn't enter the phone number for his school counselor, blank spaces showed laziness.)

While the media, the college-obsessed, and admissions officers themselves gave lots of attention to big-ticket items, the details spoke volumes. (In rare cases, they would also help us expose the cheaters.)* It was clear students knew the importance of testing, transcripts, and essays. But the application process gave advantages to students who capitalized on every opportunity. In a process where so few students were admitted, the little things could matter.

"So, are you checking social media?" the young man asked. "I mean, it's not like you can see our Instagram if you don't have permission."

---

* Cheating was seemingly rare in our pool. But sometimes small details, such as regular grammar mistakes in a short answer, would tip us that an otherwise "perfect" application was fraudulent. We worked hard to double-check sources if a recommendation seemed suspicious. We required "official" standardized testing submitted from the College Board before matriculation. And we opened our phone lines for anonymous tips about application fraud.

Toward the end of my career, I received more and more social media questions. And in this case, it was clear to me that this student had thought long and hard about the topic. (It made me wonder how many pictures of him underage drinking were publicly available online.) "We reserve the right to check," I responded.

"But you're not, right?"

I didn't have time to google students. Nor did I have much interest. However, occasionally I'd google a student to prove that he really did win the Cockapoo Comedy Award (and to find out exactly what the Cockapoo Comedy Award was). Rarely, I'd google an applicant to make sure that his accolades were authentic. But most of the time, I couldn't be bothered. But I didn't want students thinking they shouldn't worry about their online presence. "It's fair game," I insisted.

"So, that's a no?" the student pressed.

"It's a yes," I exaggerated-slash-lied. "Yes, I do. So you should clean it up. Not just for college but for yourselves."

I was overly dramatic. These students shouldn't have needed a lecture from me. The threat of a college admissions officer googling a student should have been reason enough to delete the picture of him doing you-know-what at you-know-who's. Cleaning up one's online profile was more about decency than college preparedness.

And while the odds were against social-media checking, it could happen. (Alumni interviewers would occasionally google applicants so they could recognize them in a coffee shop. One of my more social-media-obsessed colleagues occasionally checked on applicants who bragged about their number of social media followers. And I *had* googled about ten students—out of thousands—in my career.) In a process that was already so competitive, it only made sense to mind one's lesser foot, while still putting one's best foot forward.

Mistakes happen. When I read applications, I'd forgive students for the occasional blunder. (I was especially forgiving to students who indicated that they completed their applications with limited access to the internet and computers.)* The errant spelling mistake was fine. The wrong testing date for the SATs was forgiven.

But if a student didn't invest time in his application, then we usually didn't have reason to invest in his admission. Laziness on an application usually hurt an applicant not because the admissions committee held it against him, but because other students took advantage of the opportunity. As a reader, I wasn't going to care if a student neglected to list his senior spring curriculum. But another student who listed the strength of his classes made his own case stronger.

"But another student from my school was admitted and I wasn't," Jessie, a denied applicant, said as she spoke over the phone. "I'm a much better student."

It was natural for students to compare themselves to other students in their school. In this case, the woman on the phone *was* the stronger student in terms of academic GPA. But we weren't comparing an apple to an apple; we were comparing an apple to an apple field. Jessie's apple hadn't appeared as shiny. I couldn't tell her this, of course. "Unfortunately, we can't speak of other applicants in the pool."

"Well, can you tell me what I did wrong?"

I peeked at her application.† My own words stared back at me on the page. They read something like the following:

Jessie is third in her class at a competitive high school. Recommenders describe her as a leader on the softball field and in the

---

* I remember one counselor from South Africa arguing that her students were completing applications on cell phones that they borrowed from their teacher. Each was given a limited amount of time to apply. It broke my heart and made me more sympathetic to occasional application mistakes.

† As I've mentioned before, we weren't supposed to peek into an application. But I'd look when I needed to.

humanities classrooms. Her essay gives us an insight into her interest in literature as a way to connect peoples. But overall application falls flat in pool.

"Flat" was all I needed to write on an application summary for the next reader to understand my sentiment. "Flat" meant exactly how it sounded: void of depth. Jessie wrote a standard application. She didn't write a single word more than was required. She didn't submit the peer recommendation. She didn't provide much insight to make her case. Her application was like many others.

"We're not allowed to comment on our decisions, but I can assure you that there was no single thing that determined our decision," I shared.

"I want to apply next year as a transfer student," she continued. "Can you give me some advice?"

I could. I could tell Jessie that she should have written her short answer about something other than teamwork. (As the captain of the softball team, she should have known about teamwork.) I could tell her that she should have filled out an additional information section with a comment on choosing to repeat freshman year as she transferred schools. (It was mentioned briefly by her counselor.) I could tell her that she should have written more about having eight (!) siblings. I could tell her that she should have told us more about S.C.O.R.E. (whatever that was), which was listed as her activity with her greatest time commitment.

But I didn't. "Keep your grades up," I offered unhelpfully.

I didn't have the heart to tell a student that her application lacked depth. I wasn't confident that even if we did know more about Jessie she would have been admitted. I didn't want to make her feel badly about her application presentation. And it wasn't my place. (As I've mentioned, we weren't supposed to comment on the strengths or weaknesses of any application.)

But I would preach to anyone who hadn't yet pressed the send button. Spellchecking is obvious. Proofreading is necessary. Waiving one's rights to review recommendations is important as it proves to the reviewer than an applicant isn't confining recommenders to only positive commentary.* But the students who positioned themselves for the best possible application outcomes are those who took time to fill in every blank. With thoroughness, a "flat" application could become an application of depth. With strategy, a repetitive application could become a multidimensional application. With elbow grease, a standard application could become a standout application.

Applying to colleges is often a student's first exercise in self-marketing. It's good practice for the real world. (Just try convincing one's future employer that those questionable Instagram photos don't matter.) It's an opportunity for self-reflection (and finding out exactly what your mother does for a living). And in my opinion, it's a small amount of work considering the payoff.

There are no guarantees of admission. College admissions is a business, and colleges admit the students they need and deny the ones they don't need, despite how well written one's application is. There's no reason to obsess over every single word. (Too many edits will spoil a perfectly good essay.) There are no magic application formulas. (Anyone who says otherwise should be reported to the authorities.) And there is no such thing as a *perfect* application.

But there should be no regrets. There should be no missed opportunities. There should be no "if onlys." And there should never, ever, be immature e-mail addresses.

---

* In my opinion, making admissions officers wonder why a student wouldn't waive his rights was never a good move. (My imagination was far too juicy.)

CHAPTER THIRTEEN

ALUMNI INTERVIEWS

After an application is submitted, there is still one final hurdle for many college-bound students: the interview. Many colleges offer some sort of interview for their applicants. Some offer on-campus admissions officer interviews. Some offer virtual interviews with current students. And still others offer interviews with folks ranging from admissions senior fellows to campus deans. (I suggest that a student contact a college directly for interview policies and procedures.)

Alumni interviews tend to be the most popular interview offering at highly selective colleges. As colleges and universities received more applications, it only made sense to deploy alumni to help with the interviewing process. (I've always been impressed with the University of Pennsylvania, which was able to offer over 90 percent of their applicants an alumni interview.)

At Dartmouth, we relied solely on alumni interviews. (Even though I read thousands of interview reports, I personally never interviewed an applicant living in the United States.)* We relied on students from our past to help us shape the class of the future. And from conversations with colleagues, many of our competitor schools conducted and considered their alumni interviews similarly. Many of us shared the same ground rules.

A PROSPECTIVE STUDENT COULDN'T BE INTERVIEWED BY AN ALUM UNTIL HER APPLICATION WAS DEEMED COMPLETE.

---

* I occasionally interviewed applicants in remote, foreign locations.

No college wanted to waste time and resources on prospective students who were never going to submit their transcripts.

ALUMNI INTERVIEWS WERE ONLY OFFERED IN PUBLIC PLACES.

For security reasons, most colleges didn't allow folks to interview in private homes. (Dartmouth should have received a commission from Starbucks.) Safety came first. (Although I had to chuckle at some of the locations chosen for these interviews. Outside the pop-up "Santa's Workshop" in the mall had to be distracting.)

INTERVIEWS WERE NOT ALWAYS GUARANTEED.

Most colleges have limited interviewer resources for the many applications they receive. In the case of alumni interviews, schools often assigned interviews based on the location and availability of their active alumni interviewers. At Dartmouth, alumni interviews were offered based on the availability of interviewers in a student's zip code. (Some zip codes had more active alumni than others.)

Every year we admitted students without interviews. We wouldn't fault a student because she wasn't offered an interview. (Although turning down an interview leaves in question the applicant's seriousness about her candidacy. If there's a relevant concern, an applicant should e-mail the admissions office directly to explain the circumstances.) A student who was not offered an interview could still show personality through various components of the application (particularly through recommendations and writing samples). And at Dartmouth, the additional "Peer Recommendation" provided an alternative for sharing second-person commentary.

But we took the interview experience seriously. We cared about the interactions between those who had graduated and those who had not yet been admitted. We were curious how a student engaged with a stranger. And we read *every* alumni interview report.

Evaluative alumni interview policies for college admissions are not without controversy. Folks challenge their purpose, noting that the practice seems outdated and political. But for all the hullaballoo, I found the interviewing process to be quite charitable and relevant. Typically, an interview wouldn't tip the scales. But it could hold applicants accountable.

In my time at Dartmouth, I learned that both participants in an alumni interview were trying to impress the admissions office. Alumni wanted to assist us in making decisions. Students wanted to gain admission through their performance. Both interviewers and interviewees wanted to know what we were looking for in an interview evaluation. I had three answers: confirmation, expansion, and humanity.

Interviews confirmed what was already mentioned in the application. (*Chelsea's passion for Florida reptiles was obvious and contagious.*)

Interviews allowed students to expand on application information. (*Chelsea pointed out a friendship bracelet "she'd been wearing for four months," gifted to her from her ten-year-old stepsister, of whom she is a primary caregiver.*)

Interviews allowed students to be human. (*When Chelsea received the wrong order from the barista, she kept the drink without complaint, despite the barista's offer to make a new one. "No sense wasting milk," she commented.*)

Interviews were twofold. They were an opportunity for students to insert themselves into an otherwise (electronic) paper process. And they were a way to keep the alumni body engaged with a college. As a business, a college could gain extra bang for its buck by connecting prospective students with alumni.

Of course, the process had its challenges. Some families didn't believe our assignments were based on the randomness of interviewer availability. (Now and then, a parent would insist that another applicant had been preselected for an interview, even though we didn't have the interest or the bandwidth for anything but random assignments.) We didn't personally know most of the folks conducting the interviews. (We appointed a regional head interviewer to keep an eye out for creeps.) And interview write-ups weren't always the most helpful. (We did our best to help interviewers do their best. We provided training documents, resources, and sample summaries.)

But our biggest problem with alumni interviews was our biggest blessing. For the most part, interviews seemed to go well. (Alumni were not privy to any pieces of the application, so their experiences were based solely on their personal interactions.) Alumni tended to recommend most of their interviewees. The positive interviews far outweighed the negatives. And both interviewees and interviewers seemed to enjoy the experience. But all this positivity didn't always help us make decisions.

"They're just all so darn amazing," the head of an alumni interviewing club said to me between bites of pad Thai. "I honestly don't know how you make your decisions."

"It's not easy." I smiled.

"Not easy? It's darn near impossible." He leaned in. "I personally interviewed five kids last year. All five knocked my socks off. You took none of them."

"We wait-listed three," I said with an apologetic grin.

"Well, at least that counts for something." He laughed. "If keeping kids out of the deny bin and onto the wait list is the best I can do, then I'll take it." He took a sip of a beer and leaned back. "Honestly, Becky, I don't know what else these kids need to do to gain admission."

This was a regular theme of my conversations with alumni interviewers. Everyone was impressive. Everyone was deserving. Everyone should have been admitted.

As part of my job, I met with coordinating heads of alumni interview

clubs. I met with Tennessee interviewers over barbecue. I met with Louisiana interviewers over beignets. I met with California interviewers over
vegan matcha green tea lattes with agave syrup.

What I learned from these conversations is that there are differing
opinions on what's best for the college. Some alumni are hell-bent on
preserving college traditions; others are desperate to see change. Some
are frustrated with college leadership; some are its biggest supporters.
Some champion *Keggy the Keg* as the unofficial mascot of the college;
some want to see him kicked.

The one thing the alumni body had in common was their amaze-
ment with our young people.

Even the strongest proponent of the arts could appreciate the talent of a young engineer.

Even a conservative southerner could champion a liberal New
England transplant to Atlanta.

Even a passionate sorority alumna could recommend a student
with no interest in Greek life.

Nearly all interviewers were able to put their biases aside in order to
marvel at the talent of the future. And rarely but wonderfully, an alum
would grow from an interaction with one of these young people. (*"After
my conversation with Joy, I found myself, too, asking for paper straws."*)
Yet interviews that were generally positive didn't tip the scales as signifi-
cantly as negative interviews.

"Next year, I hope I can interview someone who isn't so incredible." The
alumnus chuckled. "It would make me feel more discerning."

He had a point. "Not recommended" interviews were rare. (My colleagues at competing institutions agreed with this sentiment.) The truth

was that the not-so-great interviews tended to make a larger impact than most of the positive ones because they were so infrequent. (We considered context when considering all interviews. If a negative interview summary arrived, we'd sniff around for foul play before using the rating.)

When evaluating an interview, we found some behaviors were inexcusable. It was significant to know that a student was late without reason or apology. (Rudeness counted.) It was helpful to hear that a student didn't have much to say about his so-called academic passion. (Introversion was perfectly acceptable. Disengagement was unflattering.) It was telling if an interviewee and his application had striking dissimilarities. (Frankly, some interview summaries helped us eventually discover fraudulent applicants.)

Of course, *extraordinary* interviews could help applicants. (I'd revisit an application in the deny bin if his interview rating was extraordinary, just to make sure I hadn't missed anything.) Interviewers could help us understand the motivations, inspirations, and personality that sometimes faded on paper. A student who wowed his interviewer would certainly receive a second look from our reviewers. And an outstanding interview made an applicant a little harder to deny.

As an example of a possible alumni evaluation:

Herbert Gordon was very knowledgeable about the current local election in Fayetteville. Without spilling who he'd vote for, he talked about what mattered to him in a campaign (green space, solar energy, and public transportation). I found his knowledge of our local political system incredibly high level for a high school student (and I walked away convinced by him that we need to refinance our public libraries).

What stood out most to me was the number of people (of diverse ages and backgrounds) who recognized him in the small coffee shop. (We were regularly interrupted by someone wanting to say hi.) As I'm sure you've seen in his application, he's involved in an array of activities. But sitting in a corner coffee shop, it was clear that Herbert's most important activity is interacting with Fayetteville's people. He'd be an outstanding addition to the Dartmouth community, both for his brain and for his heart.

Herbert's interview spoke to the person. It brought a new dimension to his candidacy. And while the admissions committee might have known about his environmental science and political passions, the interview made these interests come alive.

Sometimes, the interview's success seemed to be dependent on the talent and friendliness of the interviewer. (Oprah could have made any prospective student look good.) Great interviewers could tease out more from a person than we could tease out from an application. One interviewer asked students what they'd miss most about home if they moved away to college. (This showed what mattered to them and why.) Another asked which living celebrity/author/writer/musician/artist the student would admit to the college and why. (Ruth Bader Ginsburg and Beyoncé made the list for similar reasons.) Some interviewers asked about favorite teachers. (This question turned the teacher recommendation on its head.) And one interviewer asked what a student would do if she didn't go to college. (I loved this question as it reflected on a student's thoughtfulness around plan B, which many students clearly never considered.)

But all interviews could offer some perspective. An articulate student could make the most of any conversation, no matter how dull an interviewer's questions. (Introverts also need not worry provided they appeared engaged and curious.) And while it's hard to instruct a high school student how to interview well, there are ways (beyond the basics) * to make an interview better.

My best tips for interviewees are:

---

* Show up on time. Send a thank-you. Ask well-researched questions. Don't slurp.

1. Bring a résumé.

Most colleges instruct interviewers not to ask about standardized test scores or GPAs. (I think it's fine for the student to share this information if comfortable.) But a résumé can help jump-start an alum's memory when she is writing up the interview later. While many admissions officers rarely want résumés, alumni interviewers seemed happy to accept them. Leaving a résumé as a paper trail can only help them remember a student in a sea of interviewees. (*Was Petra or Penelope the diver who came straight from the pool, smelling of chlorine and competition?*)

2. Show something the application won't tell.

Yes, Charlotte loves her saxophone. Yes, she's a forensics whiz. Chances are these activities are going to blanket her entire application. But if she wants to share something else, this is an opportunity. (*"Although I didn't talk about baking in my application, I'd love for you to share my recent win at the Pumpkin Pie Palooza with the admissions committee."*)

3. Ask the alum about the alumni experience.

Alumni love to talk. It could be dangerous to ask an alum too many questions about her glory days, especially with limited time. But it can be valuable to ask the interviewer about her experience as an alumna of the college. Is the alumni body active in one's hometown? Are there special events they host? Do they recruit students for internships, jobs, etc.? A student should use this time to learn more about the college, in addition to allowing the interviewer to learn more about him.

4. Tell them how much you enjoyed the conversation.

Interviewers volunteer their time because they find prospective students interesting. Even if an interview wasn't perfect, it's important for a student to tell the alum that his time is appreciated. (On a serious note, if a student is concerned about any inappropriate comments, discussions, or situations during an interview, he should reach out to the admissions office for a confidential conversation.) By showing the interviewer that the student enjoyed himself, the interviewer will feel better about the entire experience. Positivity breeds positivity.

Interviews, at their heart, are an attempt to add a human element to an otherwise inhumane process. They (hopefully) allow both participants to take a little something, give a little something, and laugh a little along the way. They are designed to allow both participants to be the good guys. And while they are self-serving for the college (in engaging both alumni and prospective students), they are well intentioned.

I loved meeting with our alumni interviewers. I enjoyed listening to them marvel about our young people. ("Apparently, they're good for more than fixing my phone," one senior alum joked with me.) And I hoped that our prospective students walked away from these experiences on a positive note.

If nothing else, an alumni interview is a useful real-world experience. (Isn't the purpose of college to prepare for the real world, anyway?) Interviewees should be excited. They should be nervous. They should take it seriously. And they should send the handwritten thank-you note.

This is a moment to engage with a stranger. This is an opportunity to present oneself in person, not just on paper. This is a chance to discuss ideas, events, and plastic straws with someone who *wants* to be there.

And of all the admissions hurdles there are to jump, an interview might be the most relevant in preparing for life after high school.

SPECIAL CONSIDERATIONS

CHAPTER FOURTEEN

A WORD ON EARLY

Students loved to tell me that they were applying early to Dartmouth. It was their badge of honor, a reflection of their organizational skills and their commitment to the college. We were ecstatic to accept their applications (especially since we had much more time in November to review candidates than we did in January).

"I just hope applying early helps my chances," Mary said during my visit to her high school. "Dartmouth has been my first choice all along, and if submitting an application before November gives me an advantage, I'll take it!"

Most applicants to college still apply through regular decision. Yet one's admissions odds can be better with an early application. At many competitive colleges (including Dartmouth), there is a statistical advantage in the process, even if it's slight. (Dartmouth and many other colleges admit most of their recruited athletes early. This special group of preselected athletes bumped the overall admit rate to a misleading number. But in this case and many others, even when recruited athletes are removed from the equation, nonathletes are still advantaged statistically in the early process.) *

The opportunity to better one's odds is tempting. (As a Vegas vacation gambler, I know the importance of knowing when to hold 'em and when to fold 'em.) But as a high school student, I didn't quite understand the benefits of early decision. At my public school, few of my peers were

---

* As the main liaison for athletic recruitment at Dartmouth, I spent many hours explaining these numbers.

applying early, and few of my mentors were encouraging it. (Frankly, early programs seemed reserved for students with special considerations, including athletes and donor-interest candidates.) I never understood the pros and cons of early programs until I worked in the admissions office.

Early programs have always been controversial. Some colleges lean on them strongly to shape their classes (and arguably act favorably toward legacy candidates). Some colleges depend on early admission numbers to allow for lower overall admissions rates. (The schools who can admit a larger early decision class can admit a smaller regular decision class, often leading to an overall lower admit rate.) And some schools might soon attract early candidates with special scholarships or housing priorities. (The business of college admission is becoming quite competitive, folks.)

And in my experience, well-resourced high schools are better prepared to handle early applications. (They have more counseling support and more experience with completing applications before November.) Students at less-resourced schools might have a disadvantage in filing an application before the standard due date. (One student complained to me that her teachers weren't in any rush to complete early recommendations.)

Still, early programs could be incredibly advantageous. (Of course, I encourage students to research a college's early policies before applying.) * While I worked at Dartmouth, a student's statistical best chance at admission was with an early application. But before one signed an early program contract, it was critical to recognize the difference between programs. (There are various derivatives of early programs, but early decision and early action are the most popular.)

---

* For example, early admitted students to Dartmouth weren't typically invited to our spring admitted student events. Although we'd provide transportation funding to these events for regular decision students who qualified financially, early decision admits would receive no transportation funding to campus. They were on their own if they wanted to visit.

Early decision programs are binding agreements with a college, assuring the school that an applicant will matriculate if accepted.

Early action programs are nonbinding agreements with a college, allowing a student to receive his decision before others but not requiring him to matriculate.

Early action is clearly the sexier of the two options. Early action provides admissions assurance without the commitment. But binding early decision programs can offer stronger statistical admissions advantages as colleges hope to lock down students before reviewing their regular pools.

Early programs allow students the relief of college admission far earlier than their regular decision peers. (Most early program decisions are released in mid-December, whereas regular decisions aren't released until the end of March.) Early programs aren't for everyone, though. There can be real issues with applying early.

1. **Early decision doesn't allow a student to compare multiple financial aid awards.**

This is an unfair reality for many college-bound students. Binding early programs only allow a student to consider one institution's financial aid package (if admitted). At many schools, the financial aid offices will work to make sure all options have been utilized for their early students. Still, there are many cases where colleges can't match other offers. (For example, a student applying to a need-based institution won't be able to consider merit-based scholarships from other schools.) However, in my experience, colleges and universities will allow students to be released from their ED agreements if tuition is not attainable by a family even after a financial aid award appeal.

2. **Late bloomers' applications might not be as strong without senior midyear grades.**

While most early decision programs consider first-quarter or first-trimester grades (providing they are submitted by late November), midyear grades usually aren't available before early decisions are made. Students with weaker junior-year grades prosper from having strong first-term grades senior year as part of their consideration.

3. **A student needs to identify a first-choice school by early November.**

Decisions, decisions! If a student hasn't had the chance to visit his potential ED choice, or simply identify his front-runner, he might be hesitant to commit to a binding program.

Other issues with early programs might be the competitiveness of one's early pool. (Although in my experience, Dartmouth's early pool was similarly competitive to the regular pool.) Or the inability to submit a complete application by November. (Early application deadlines are usually about two months earlier than regular decision deadlines. But I believe getting one's ducks in a row earlier doesn't seem like a big sacrifice for students looking for advantages.) Plus, I witnessed some early decision students who fell victim to "senioritis" (i.e., putting less effort into one's schoolwork after being admitted). Many colleges reserve the right to rescind admission at any time during senior year for academic or other reasons. (I witnessed a handful of cases every year where an early admitted student was in hot water because of plummeting grades or disciplinary actions.)

Also, if a student is deferred, his application will be re-reviewed in the regular pool. (Most colleges admit, defer, or deny students in their early pools.) Although a deferred student's midyear transcript will be submitted to the college, the student should also submit his own e-mail update with any relevant new activities/awards/passions. (And *"College X continues to be my first choice"* is always helpful to include.) While admissions officers silently cheer for deferrals (since we hope students who have declared our institution their first choice are admitted), it's often a tough and competitive road for those who weren't originally admitted. (At Dartmouth, our deferral-to-admit rate was approximately the same as the overall regular decision admit rate.)

I support students who decide to apply somewhere early, providing they are aware of the fine print. (And I applaud the conversations about equalizing the "early" playing field for students who rely on financial aid comparisons.) I hope that these applicants keep their second-choice colleges in their hearts (as the majority will not end up at their preferred early institution). And I keep my fingers crossed that they ask their teachers for recommendations with more than one week of advance notice. (Let's be compassionate, folks.)

Early programs have their perks. But they also provide their pressures. It's up to an individual to realistically weigh the advantages and disadvantages of applying early. And it's up to colleges to better advertise, implement, and provide equal opportunity for those interested in these programs.

CHAPTER FIFTEEN

INTERNATIONAL APPLICANTS

It can be tricky to live in Frankfurt and apply to college in the United States. It can be challenging to find a testing center in a Latin American country. It can be frustrating to figure out which financial aid paperwork to complete as a Nigerian citizen at a Connecticut boarding school. But international admissions officers are there to help.

As the director of international admissions, I was tasked with managing the recruitment, admission, and yield of a globally diverse class to Dartmouth. I understood that international students strengthened our campus community. I knew they elevated academic discussions in the classrooms. I recognized that they increased the cultural, linguistic, and religious diversity of the student body. And if nothing else, I was sure they'd offer Jane from Kansas City an amazing spring break opportunity to visit her British roommate's home in London.

When contemplating a college's international admissions process, there are two critical questions to consider from the start.

1. **Who is considered an international applicant?**
Because of college financial aid policies, the term "international applicant" is defined carefully by colleges and universities. At Dartmouth, we defined an "international applicant" in our reporting as one who did not hold a U.S. passport. (Permanent residents, eligible noncitizens, and undocumented students were exceptions to this rule and reviewed in the same process as American citizens.) U.S. citizens living in Australia were not counted in "international" numbers. Australian citizens living in Nebraska were counted.

2. **Does an international applicant's need for financial aid factor into his admissions decision? (And is there financial aid available to those who qualify?)**

Most colleges in the United States, including Dartmouth, are need-aware for students without U.S. citizenship, which means that they consider a student's ability to pay tuition when making admissions decisions. (When I began working at the college, we had a *need-blind* policy toward all applicants. In the fall of 2015, our policy changed to *need-aware* for those without U.S. passports.)* Need-aware schools like Dartmouth, which meet full financial need, must separate students by citizenship because of financial aid policies. (Noncitizens do not receive United States financial aid grant money, forcing colleges to cover the gap.) Wealthier students are easier to admit as schools have limited budgets for international financial aid. Yet most colleges are committed to achieving socioeconomic diversity within their international pools, so they do their best to stretch their dollars.

Regardless of our financial aid policies, the international admissions process at Dartmouth was painfully more competitive than our (already painstakingly competitive) domestic review. During my time on campus, our international admission rate was around 2 percent. (On average, we received around four thousand applications from students with foreign citizenships. We would admit about ninety of these students per year.) Approximately 6 to 10 percent of each class held foreign passports. A number of these spots were reserved for recruited athletes.† The other slots had to be carefully balanced among many countries in order to maintain diversity of citizenships.

---

* Dartmouth protected permanent residents, eligible noncitizens, and undocumented students in the United States under our need-blind policy. I strongly suggest that those who fall in these categories contact colleges of interest to clarify their policies.

† We recruited our fair share of Canadian hockey players.

The diversity of the international pool required special care. These applications were reviewed by experienced counselors and managed closely. We received applications from metropolitan Asian cities, rural European villages, Pacific Island nations, and South American suburbs. Applicants spoke various languages, attended schools with differing academic expectations, and partook in very different (and sometimes very few) extracurricular activities. They were courageous, educationally focused, and adventurous in their quests to study abroad.

Recruiting internationally was a thrill of a lifetime. In the span of my career, I recruited in places such as Thailand, Costa Rica, Brazil, Norway, Wales, Swaziland, Tanzania, Taiwan, and Panama. And no recruitment trip was the same. In São Paulo, I carefully explained and defended the meaning of a liberal arts diploma. In Johannesburg, I defined what it meant to have a college *major*. In Singapore, I spoke with expats who wondered how their children would be reviewed as U.S. citizens abroad. In London, I fielded questions from skeptical students who wondered if a Dartmouth education could compete with the likes of Oxford or Cambridge.

With a 2 percent admissions rate, I didn't believe we needed as many weeks on the road as we spent. (We visited fancy Korean schools with English language programs for the same reason we visited fancy American privates: we knew there was always potential for more applications.) But I understood the college's need for global boots on the ground. During my overseas trips as director of international admissions,* I met with alumni interviewers to thank them for their volunteer hours (especially since we admitted so few of their interviewees). I visited some questionable schools to sniff out fraud. (We wanted to ensure that schools sending us multiple strong applications were as impeccable as they

---

* On my first professional international recruiting trip, a dean sent me on a two-and-a-half-week tour of Asia. Before that trip, I'd only been out of the country a handful of times. The entirety of my days spent abroad did not equal the amount of time I'd be traveling through Asia.

seemed.) I met with local nonprofit administrators to understand the concerns, trends, and victories of their students heading abroad. (EducationUSA, a U.S. Department of State organization active in nearly 170 countries, was a common resource on the road.) And I traveled with colleagues from similar institutions for safety, financial, and marketing reasons. (My standing Asia travel group included peers from the University of Chicago, Duke, Stanford, Wellesley, and Yale. To this day, some of these travel partners remain some of my closest friends.)

In many countries, we didn't have to sell our universities. International recruitment was a clear example of how rankings mattered when it came to students wanting to find jobs at home. (It was clear that "top-ranked" universities had an upper hand in recruiting abroad because students wanted to be sure they were employable with their American degrees.) Most international students were comfortable with the idea of an American diploma and knew employers in their home countries would find these degrees valuable. They wanted in. (Recruiting on a group trip in Seoul was the closest I'd feel to being a rock star. Students were maniacal about face time with us. Yale was the Paul McCartney of our travel group, with a never-ending line of people just waiting to say hello. Dartmouth was more of a Ringo.)

Yet wherever I was and whoever I was with, I knew the chance of admission was bleak for any international student. Even the sharpest applicant from India or the sole applicant from Ireland would be up against incredible odds at most competitive U.S. colleges. (And yes, a sole applicant from any country would have a slight advantage over an applicant from an overrepresented country. But we turned away many "sole applicants" as they still had *intense* competition.) For most of these students, their chances were less favorable if they couldn't afford to pay full tuition.

Whether colleges were need-blind or need-aware, there were unspoken limitations on how many international citizens we'd have in the class. We were an American-centric institution with approximately 90 percent of the class holding U.S. passports. International students, while highly valued by the college community, would still be a minority of the class.

But with nearly unlimited application potential in global markets (and the economic assurance of full-pay students), many colleges are still looking overseas. Colleges will differ on their policies and procedures in recruiting these students. Some are aggressive in their marketing toward foreigners. Others don't have the budgets for travel abroad. But there certainly is interest in talented students from nations near and far. And clever international students can give themselves an advantage in the application process in a few specific ways.

1. Put schooling into context for the reader.

At many competitive colleges and universities, the regional admissions officer for a student's *school geographic location* reviews the application first. At Dartmouth, for example, the following two students would be read in this order:

> Hayley, who attended school in Japan and held a U.S. passport, would first be considered by the admissions officer responsible for East Asia. Her second review would be completed by an officer who considered all U.S. citizens living abroad.

> Purnell, who attended a school in Chicago and held a Nigerian passport, would first be reviewed by the admissions officer responsible for Chicago. His second review would be completed by the officer who considered Africa.

The regional admissions officer would learn a country's general schooling principles. (As the first reader for all students schooled in China, I became very comfortable with the gaokao exam.) And many domestic and international admissions counselors were familiar with the widely popular International Baccalaureate curriculum and its predicted grades. But it was helpful when students submitted an explanation of their school's specific curriculum, their extracurricular offerings,* and their general ethos (if relevant). If a school offers no after-school activities, a student should share this information. If a school requires every student to take a national exam, a student should share general details about the test. There's no such thing as overexplanation, and international admissions reviewers will appreciate contextual background.

2. **Recognize that the "school counselor" recommendation doesn't need to be completed by a traditional school counselor.**

Most international schools don't offer school counselors in the American sense. I read required counselor recommendations from headmasters, English teachers, and nonprofit organization tutors. We didn't need a rec from a "school counselor," but we needed a recommendation from someone who could provide an overview of the applicant's coursework, curriculum, and overall student experience.

3. **Take testing requirements seriously.**

Often, international students have limited opportunities for taking standardized tests. (If testing is not offered in a student's home country, many colleges will waive the testing requirement.)[†] I found that students living overseas needed to be more organized when it came to application materials. In addition to regular testing requirements, English-language proficiency tests (i.e., the TOEFL, the IELTS exam, the Duolingo English Test) are often recommended for non-native English speakers applying from international countries. (At Dartmouth, students who were schooled in English weren't required to submit these

---

* European schools famously didn't offer a laundry list of extracurricular activities in the same way as U.S. high schools. We'd recognize that an applicant might not have the opportunity to edit yearbook superlatives in the same way as American students.

† Interestingly, the SAT test is not offered in China. However, most Chinese applicants submitted scores from test centers in Taiwan, Hong Kong, Singapore, and other countries.

tests.) As unfair as it may be, often standardized testing carries greater weight with international application review, as it helps to confirm a student's language comprehension and overall academic preparedness for the college. (In a few cases where international applicants' transcripts were difficult to decipher, standardized testing became that much more important.)

Admissions offices recognized the challenges international students faced as they completed Americanized applications. But in my experience, most colleges would be flexible with their requirements, providing a student shared her challenges. (For example, we'd allow students to translate their own recommendations if there was no other option.) Once students matriculated, we were also happy to connect them and our international student advisor to assist with students' specific needs.

I worked to keep in touch with some of our international students throughout their four years of college. I met many of them at the first-year international student welcome.* I helped some acclimate to campus life during their first year. (During a memorable Walmart shopping trip with two special international scholarship students, I was humiliated when I suggested both buy the same jacket, pants, and shirt. "With respect, ma'am, we don't want to establish a scholarship kid's uniform," one responded politely. Lesson learned.) I invited them to "drop in" for tootsie roll pops and conversation in my office as they became upper-classmen. And toward the end of their college careers, I'd host them for dinners of (sadly unimpressive) homemade lasagna.

But as I came to know these students, their circumstances, and the countries they called home, I realized that many of them wanted to be known on campus for themselves, not their country.

---

* In my speech one year, I translated the cost of the local "pizza special" into currency from every represented country in the class. It might have been irrelevant, but it fostered a lot of smiles from the audience. Pizza, it seemed, was universal.

"I don't want to defend Turkey's political choices just because I'm the Turkish student in the class," one student shared with me over dinner at my home. "I just want to be a college student, not the Turkish student."

"Do you know how hard it is being the only student in my class from New Zealand?" another student lamented in my office.

"As much as I love the idea of living in the Global Village dorm, I'm here to be more than an international student," still another announced.

It wasn't a new sentiment. This was a common concern from many young people stigmatized by their campus category. Athletes wanted to be more than athletes. Nonbinary students wanted to be more than their gender. Legacies wanted to be more than their parents' shadows. At the end of the day, our young people wanted to be valued for their individual perspectives and not just the perspectives of the boxes they checked in an admissions report.

But in reading international applications, admissions officers paid attention to citizenship (and often ability to pay). Schools were under pressure to top the number of countries from the previous class. ("*This year, we have forty-two countries represented in our incoming first-year class, up from forty in years prior.*") Universities wanted to increase the number of foreign citizens in their school profiles. And everyone wanted to appease global alumni by representing their countries in our classes.

Admissions officers know that an international student is more than his citizenship. Lumping international students into one category is insane. Some attend U.S. boarding schools for nearly all their lives. Some never leave their home countries. (One student didn't drink liquids for an entire day on his journey to Dartmouth because, as a first-time flier, he didn't know airplanes had lavatories.) Some have family who purchase apartments near campus. Some can't afford the application fee. We did our best to review international applicants for who they were, not which boxes they checked. But because of financial aid pressures, Dartmouth and many other institutions had to pay attention to qualities outside a student's control (ability to pay and citizenship). It was unfair, certainly, but it was common practice.

The best an international student can do is be realistic about his ability to pay tuition when filling out admissions and financial aid forms. (Often, if a student doesn't check the application box for financial aid, he won't later be able to apply for aid if admitted.) He can research American colleges that offer strong support for students from global locations. He can ask important questions of international admissions officers and be his own advocate when filling out the schooling section of an application.

International students are unique and varied in their perspectives. In *the* most competitive admissions pool at many colleges, they have found their way to campus. Their applications often possess something that a college craves in its profile, in its community, in its classroom. No matter why they are admitted and no matter where they come from, they become one of the many. And colleges like Dartmouth become *their* study abroad programs. How fortunate for us.

CHAPTER SIXTEEN

RECRUITED ATHLETES

The coach sat in the wooden chair in my office. He handed me a manila folder. It was filled with application pieces for his priority recruit. "He's really got a foot on him. He'll likely be the top scorer in the league next year."

The recruit may have been able to kick. But it was my job to make sure he could write.

For most of my career, I was the primary admissions liaison to the athletics department. (I oversaw a handful of admissions colleagues who also worked with athletic recruits.) I met regularly with coaches who reserved a number of admissions slots for their "top talent." (Some coaches' recruiting lists were more diverse than others.) I spent time with Ivy League admissions counterparts, discussing various ways to review top heavyweight rowers' international transcripts. (The transcripts from Australia always threw us for a loop.) And I read applications from high school high jumpers, midfielders, goalies, and breaststrokers without watching them run, kick, save, or swim.

Although athletes and nonathletes completed the same applications, our admissions office spent *triple* the time on athletic applications. (While Dartmouth considered applicants' athletic talent in a few non-varsity sports, including our equestrian and skating programs, only the varsity recruits' credentials were monitored by the Ivy League.) Athletic applications were unique in many ways.

1. **Each recruited athlete went through an academic preview process.**

Before an athlete applied to the college, our admissions office would review his academic materials to ensure the student met the standards of

the Ivy League Academic Index. The Academic Index, or AI, is a complicated and controversial standardized Ivy League calculation. It's derived
from a student's GPA and test scores. It involves a lot of math, sweat, and
good intentions. But it's also flawed. (For example, strength of curriculum isn't considered in this calculation.)

2. **Recruited athletes could receive "feedback" on their
   applications as early as July 1 of their rising senior year.** *

Recruited athletes didn't have to wait until late November (or late March)
to know their admissions probability. We provided coaches early feedback on their recruits of "looks good," "possible," and "unrecruitable"
before application deadlines. With the pressures of athletic recruiting,
some coaches committed (and cleared with admissions) their entire class
of recruits by August. (While many of my colleagues vacationed in July,
I sipped on mocha lattes while reviewing women's lacrosse transcripts.)
Each application (once complete) would be re-reviewed to ensure that a
student's essay, recommendation, and other application materials were
strong. (Sometimes we'd distribute "likely letters" to these athletes once
their full applications were reviewed.) But most of the time, a student
who received positive early feedback would be admitted.

3. **Coaches served as the primary contact for recruits during their
   admissions process.**

Admissions officers were prohibited from communicating directly with
recruits and their families about students' admissions status, so the
coaches were a recruited athlete's primary point of contact at the college.
While we were happy to answer an athlete's general question, all student-
specific inquiries had to be handled by a coach. Admissions spent much
time training coaches on admissions policies and procedures so that they
could be knowledgeable allies in the process.

---

* Leagues vary in their own feedback regulations and timelines.

I recognize that I worked with only one athletic league in the country. Many other athletic leagues are more complicated, more financially profitable, and more watched. (Dartmouth women's basketball wasn't exactly competing with UConn for primetime television.) Our office cared about making the athletic admissions process as equitable to the nonathletic process as possible. Spending less time on their applications would have resulted in a less-regulated admissions process. (Without calculating some sort of Academic Index, it would be hard to monitor the quality of academic students our coaches were recruiting.)

The good news was that about 90 percent of the athletes I reviewed "looked good." Most recruits had good grades (A/B+ mix) and okay test scores (within an arm's reach of the average) and were taking challenging curriculums. More importantly, they seemed to have strong recommendations from their counselors and teachers. (School support mattered, even in the numbers-driven recruitment process.)

Yes, we took student athletes who otherwise wouldn't be admitted to Dartmouth.* Many of them were academically sound young people with incredible talents in sport, even if they weren't pushing up our absurdly high standardized test score. Most athletic recruits were easy for me to vote to admit. But now and again, a recruit's materials would give pause.

"He has a C minus in gym," my colleague complained.

"And he's their top recruit?" I asked, dumbfounded.

Lucas could jump higher, run faster, and throw farther than anyone else in the Midwest. Our coaches were drooling over his athletic prowess and potential to add to their team. But he was barely passing physical education.

"The rest of his transcript is pretty decent." She shrugged.

---

* When parents confided in me that they were going to teach their kid to play squash to be admitted to Dartmouth, I wished them luck. They had no idea how darn competitive squash is at the collegiate level. (Many of our squash recruits were top junior American players.)

"I have to believe that he's just not trying." I looked at his transcript.

"Maybe he forgot his gym socks a few times," my colleague muttered. "Acing gym isn't all about running the mile."

"Right," I replied. "It's about remembering your gym socks." I huffed as I looked the transcript up and down. "And as I recall, remembering your gym socks is easier than running the mile. Let's talk it over with the coach."

"The coach doesn't seem concerned by the grade," my colleague responded. "Since his Academic Index is high, they're pretty confident we should take him."

In this case, and many others, the Academic Index didn't tell the whole story. AIs could be manipulated by savvy families who knew how to game the system. ("*Take easier classes if one's GPA is unweighted, darling.*") But the admissions office held firm that applicants needed to be reviewed in context outside of the AI. ("*Coach, why on earth is this kid taking basic level courses?*")

In this case, Lucas's AI was strong. He was a mostly A student in a solid curriculum. He clearly was preparing himself for the rigors of college. But that C− was irking me. "Tell the coach we want an explanation. We're not giving positive feedback until we know why he's mediocre in the same field giving him an advantage."

"They're not going to be happy. Apparently, he's being recruited by another Ivy as well. The pressure is on to take him."

"Well, if another Ivy is desperate for a top athlete who can barely pass gym, then they can have him. Otherwise, they'll all just have to wait until we have more information."

Athletes completed the same application as nonathletes. But the truth was it felt like a few athletes could do less. Star athletes who played sports with major audiences could have briefer supplemental essays. Olympian-level players who would shine on a national scale could have lower AP test scores. A few "game changing" priority players could misspell a word or six. Most recruited athletes completed perfectly acceptable (and often exciting) applications. But there were some folks who clearly took advantage of the process.

I understood the complexity and magnitude of the impact of college athletics on a campus. Dartmouth students and alumni didn't want to lose to another Ivy on the field because an admissions officer was angry that a student didn't remember his socks. Dartmouth development officers didn't want alumni to stop giving to the men's and women's athletic programs. And working with coaches allowed me a glimpse into their own challenges.

"I thought you'd like a sweatshirt," the coach said to me as he handed me a green hoodie.

It was two sizes too big, but I was still honored. "I'd love one," I responded as I took it from his hands.

"I like to think you're part of our team." He smiled. "And the more folks who wear Dartmouth sports gear around this town, the better."

I'd been to a few of his games on campus. I loved the sport, the fresh air, and the family-friendly dynamic of the experience. I also liked the coach and his staff. They worked tirelessly, both on the road recruiting and on the field.

Yet coaches' success was determined by the talent and good decisions of nineteen-to-twenty-one-year-old men and women. One night of underage drinking, one academic probation, one broken arm could be a game changer for a coach's career. Meanwhile, coaches also had to fill the bleachers, engage athletic alumni, and win the Ivy championships.

Coaches needed the community's support, so I attended games, meets, and matches. I rooted, rooted, rooted for the home teams. And I wore Dartmouth athletic sweatshirts with pride. (At many an airport, I'd be approached by an alum, eager to comment on my Dartmouth swag.)

I was sympathetic to the coaches and college's need for strong athletic talent to a point. The point stopped at student laziness. I wasn't impressed with the student who "didn't get around" to taking his tests before the deadline. I wasn't thrilled reading a transcript from a student whose teacher recommended him as "talented, *when motivated.*" And I struggled to have much to say about an essay that resembled a haiku. (Even a *good* haiku is not a college personal statement.)

There were times the admissions office needed to pump the brakes. We pushed back when students didn't seem academically ready for the college. (I won that fight when "the impact player of the year" wrote an essay of seven sentences, chock-full of grammatical and spelling errors.) We pushed back harder when students seemed to take their privilege for granted. (I lost the fight when a recruit received a lackluster recommendation from his school counselor.) If a student wasn't ready for the academic rigor of the college, we'd say no. If a student wasn't ready to show up to class like a grown-up, we'd say hell no.

Coaches were typically on board with our decisions. They didn't want to inherit a student who was going to flunk out of the college. They didn't want a stain on the team's academic reputation. They trusted our judgment.

But not always. In these cases, the admissions dean and the athletics head would report to the president or provost.* Admissions would make our case. (*How is this student going to excel at Dartmouth if they blew off the alumni interview?*) The athletic office would make their case. (*This student, who happens to be the NEXT BIG THING IN SPORTS, is academically prepared for Dartmouth, despite forgetting an interview appointment.*)

I learned in these moments that neither admissions nor athletics were in charge. The college was in charge. If a student could clear the AI boundaries set by the Ivy League, the president or provost would weigh the college interests while considering the impact of the student on both the field and the classroom. (Thankfully, these situations were

---

* I personally never went to the president's office with athletic recruits. An admissions dean was the only person with that much influence.

rare. I recall us bringing athletic applications to a higher-up about once or twice annually.) Sometimes admissions would win the fight. (We'd refused the young man with a weak transcript, hoping that our competing institution would make the same decision.) Sometimes athletics would win. (We'd take the young man whose personal statement was sloppy, providing he'd write another one to prove his capability.)*

But the recruit himself would win only if he was prepared to do the work both on the field and in the classroom.

The admissions side door for athletics was not a secret. Folks knew that there were different opportunities for elite athletes. (The "Varsity Blues" scandal further complicated things with criminal approaches to college admissions and recruiting. In my experience, I witnessed nothing of the sort.) But what I learned during my time working with athletic recruits was that even the most talented athlete needed to earn his respect on campus. Athletes might impress folks on the field, but they weren't going to gain the admiration of fellow students unless they pulled their weight on the boat AND in the classroom.

I believe in college athletics. I also believe that anyone with privilege in the admissions process should at least make one's best effort. Doing more when one could do less showed one's character. There is decency in giving a damn about a personal statement. There is civility in accepting the alumni interview offer and doing one's best. There is nobility in showing up to class, participating, and getting to know the professor. These things helped students not only succeed at the college level but also prepare for life after sport.

These attributes trickled down to what we were looking for in athletic recruit applications. The most important advice I gave recruited student athletes was to be a student first when it came to the application. I encouraged them to think about how they would contribute to campus if they broke an arm. I begged them to consider how a poorly

---

* The cynic in me wondered how much help he had with his rewrite.

completed application would reflect on them, their coach, and their team. (I had seen a few coaches "drop" less-necessary recruits for not completing decent applications.) And I urged them to prove their intellectual curiosity so there was no question that academics came first.

I also instructed prospective athletes to:

1. Start the process early.

It's not fair that athletic recruits need to start their process earlier. (I can't imagine being pressured to commit to a school in July of my senior summer.) It's also not fair that they *can* start their process early.* (I can't imagine being told by a coach that I was "likely" to be admitted as early as July of my senior summer. Most other students needed to wait until the following March for their decision.) I advised students looking at Ivy League schools to contact athletic coaches near the end of their sophomore year with a simple introductory e-mail and a few athletic statistics. If a student waits too long (i.e., October of her senior year), chances are a coach will have already committed his allotted slots.

2. Talk to coaches first, not admissions officers.

I know nothing about erg scores in rowing. Most admissions officers know little about RBI stats, high jump records, or wrestling weight classes. A student shouldn't ask an admissions director about her chances to make the basketball team. Instead, she should e-mail the coach.

At most colleges, potential student athletes are encouraged to contact varsity coaches for all questions regarding steps, strategies, and status. This allows coaches to have control of their own conversations with recruits, while also allowing admissions officers to be ignorant of all things pole vault.

---

* The Ivy League had many concerns about coaches recruiting students earlier and earlier in the process. We enforced a strict July 1 (before senior year) date to review application materials, although many liaisons, coaches, and alumni interested in athletics argued for us to give feedback earlier.

3. Listen. Really listen.

In my career, I met a few students who believed they were recruits but never made the coach's list. I'll never know the conversations that led them to believe they were shoo-ins. (The coaches could have misled the families.) But I can't help but believe the families heard what they wanted to hear.

Students need to listen carefully to what a coach offers, promises, and confirms. They should ask a coach to repeat details, put whatever he can in writing, and speak to a third party (i.e., school counselor) if there is any concern. (Ivy League students can also request "likely letters" for further confirmation.)

4. Do not write an essay about one's sport. No, really. Please don't.

If an applicant is a field hockey recruit, we know she loves field hockey. It's guaranteed that we will hear about her love of field hockey through-out the application. (It's usually mentioned by counselors, teachers, and any others tossing in their opinions.) So we don't need to hear about her love of the sport or any derivative story. We don't need an essay about breaking one's leg during a game. We don't need an essay about the BIG GAME. * But we'd love an essay about her part-time holiday job as a mall gift wrapper, learning to minimize paper use (with the help of geometry).

5. Take challenging courses that will prepare oneself for the rigors of college.

College is hard enough without a four-hour daily volleyball practice. I met students who were worried they wouldn't have enough study time

---

* Consider two applications from young women living in the same county. One writes her essay about the triumph of teamwork helping to win the regional softball cham-pionship. The other writes her essay about the important lesson of humility and sportsmanship during the regional softball championship. They discuss their posi-tions from different angles of the same game. While we would never compare one applicant to another, in this case, it would be hard to advance one application over another when both are so darn similar and neither essay does much to further the student's candidacy.

to be premed if they played volleyball. I met students who knew that they weren't going to pass Latin if they took the class during their sport's season.

Learning how to be a successful student athlete starts in high school. It begins with forming a solid foundation of classwork for college. And it requires strong time management skills.

Becoming the state track champion is hard. Balancing academics with athletics can be challenging. And the college athletic recruitment process can be tricky. It's critical that student athletes surround themselves with trusted support (i.e., coaches and school counselors) as they navigate the path toward the college classroom and the court or field. It's also important that they position themselves to have the strongest academic record so that their ability to play athletically is not stifled by their inability to perform academically.

College athletics have a time and a place. They foster school spirit, they encourage teamwork and wellness, and they make a lot of money for the institution. Frankly, many college athletes awe me. (Especially the goalies. I'm both impressed by and incredibly intimidated by goalies in any sport.)

They might be able to kick, but student athletes at Dartmouth gained the respect of the admissions office only if they wrote more than seven sentences on their college essay. They received our admiration only if they put their best foot forward, despite how talented their toes, how expensive their shoes, or how fancy their footwork. They deserved the extra attention we gave to their applications only if they invested time in their persons and not just their positions.

POSTDECISION

POSTDICTION

CHAPTER SEVENTEEN

DECISION DAY

Decision day is sure to bring on students' emotions. There are the good emotions. There are the bad emotions. And there are the wait list emotions. When the phone rang in the admissions office after decisions were posted, I never knew which to expect.

Ring, ring.

There were three types of phone calls I'd receive postdecision. The first were from students who wanted to thank me for our admissions decisions.* (This happened twice in my entire career.) The second was from students who wanted to know how to stand out on the wait list. (This was the most common postdecision call.) The third was from a rejected student hoping to appeal one's decision.

Usually the tone of the caller's first words would tip me off. "I need to speak with the dean of admissions," an irritated voice commanded.

"I'm sorry a dean isn't available right now, but I'm the admissions representative for your state."

"Then you're the one who made the mistake."

This forceful mother was committing one of the cardinal sins of college admissions. She was calling on her daughter's behalf. Phone calls from rejected students were never easy. But phone calls from the parents of rejected students were even more challenging. Admissions officers had limited patience for parents conducting their children's business. (Disguising

---

* Sometimes I'd add a handwritten personal note to an admit letter, congratulating the young person and inviting them to meet me on campus upon matriculation. My colleagues and I enjoyed adding a personal touch to the mailed admit packets. It was rare we'd hear back from these students, though.

one's voice to sound like one's kid was even more reprehensible, and it happened more times than one would imagine.)

But our lines were open for anyone who felt the need to vent, complain, or voice concern. (I received about twenty phone calls after every decision release.) One student's voice broke with emotion as he asked if being an undocumented student had hurt his chances. (It hadn't. Dartmouth had a welcoming position toward undocumented students.) One parent wondered if not allowing her daughter to pursue ballet ruined her Ivy dream. (Ballet had nothing to do with our decision.) One woman with a severe eating disorder questioned whether her essay, where she disclosed her disease, hurt her chances. (It absolutely did not.)

I was well trained to be polite, listen, and offer platitudes. I was also told that we never changed a decision due to a phone call. Decisions were final, no matter how long a student cried or a grandfather screamed. There was little a person could say to change our minds.*

We were instructed not to share details of our decision. (Imagine telling a father that his son wasn't admitted because his history teacher referred to him as "run-of-the-mill.") If the student (or parent) pushed enough, we'd speak to the transfer process, encouraging him or her to apply again after attending another institution. (We wouldn't mention that our transfer process was usually much more competitive than the regular undergraduate process. We had to offer *some* hope.) But we would never tell a student why he was denied. We'd apologize for the caller's disappointment, and we'd wish them best of luck with their other college options.

This mother didn't want to hear about other college options. She had called on behalf of her daughter, a denied student from a private high school, who she believed was wrongfully rejected. As with many parental conversations, I had a feeling that the parent was angrier than the

---

* If a student's materials were switched mistakenly in an application, we would revisit the case. This was a once-in-a-career event.

student about the decision. I could nearly feel the vitriol rising from my phone speaker. "She was the top student in her county, never mind the school," she shouted. "Think of what people around here will say."

I had little concern over what people in Mrs. Shoutingmatch's social circle would say. By my calculations, her daughter was seventh in her class with her unweighted GPA, seventeenth with her weighted. She wasn't a bad student, but her application hadn't risen to the top of the pool. "I'm sure she's done quite well but the competitive nature of the class—"

"I don't want to hear about the competitive nature. I want you to fix your mistake and issue an apology!"

The mother clearly wanted the apology herself. Regardless, I could only apologize for the family's disappointment. Her daughter surely was an impressive young woman. "I'm sorry that the decision didn't turn out the way—"

"I'm not going to take no for an answer."

There wasn't much for me to say. And so I didn't say much. My silence allowed Mrs. Shoutingmatch to vent. She went on and on about Girls State and All State and First State and Best in State. According to her, our admissions committees must have been filled with idiots who "wouldn't know talent if it fell into our laps." The longer she spoke, the less I sympathized with her situation. I organized the pens on my desktop while she talked and occasionally added an "um-hum" to let her know I was still on the line. *

I could have just hung up the phone. A director had advised us to simply end a call if someone was out of line. And it was clear that Mrs. Shoutingmatch was out of line. It was also clear that she hadn't often been told no.

I wasn't hanging up. It was rare to encounter *such* a dreadful parent. Most parents were disappointed. Some parents were frustrated. But a

---

* I stole this approach from my cable provider.

rare few were this rude. Mrs. Shoutingmatch was probably unlikable in other facets of her life, but this phone call was bringing out a monster. As she continued, her comments became more inflamed. *Best, best, best. Strongest, strongest, strongest. Idiots, idiots, idiots.*

After a few minutes of her mad monologue, I piped back into the conversation. "I'm sorry, Mrs. Shoutingmatch, but there's nothing else I can do at this point."

The line went quiet for a strangely long pause. "You do understand . . . ," she said slowly and dramatically, "that unless you change your decision, my daughter's going to end up at some nothing school in the middle of nowhere."

"And what school would that be?" I asked out of curiosity.

"Colby College."

At that moment, my patience for the phone call ended. Mrs. Shoutingmatch could insult me all she wanted. She couldn't insult Colby. "I'm a Colby alumna."

Silence filled the air. "I'm not saying there's anything wrong with Colby," she backpedaled. "It's just in Maine and—"

"And anyone would be lucky to attend," I interrupted.

"Look, I didn't mean to insult your school. It's just not for Missy."

I took a deep breath. "Well then, next time have Missy call, and I'd be happy to chat with her. Otherwise, I wish you and your family a happy Tuesday." I hung up the phone.

I stared at the phone for a whole two minutes, half not believing I had hung up on her, half praying Mrs. Shoutingmatch wouldn't call back. I crept out of my office and over toward the office of the dean's assistant to make sure Mrs. Shoutingmatch hadn't brought her issues elsewhere. I did a loop around the administrative assistant cubicles, listening for evidence of her call to another officer.

Mrs. Shoutingmatch never called back. There was nothing she could say. (Unsurprisingly, her daughter never called either.)

Receiving a college rejection is difficult. Nobody wants to feel shunned. (No parent wants to see her child become shunned.) I don't have great advice on how a student should process rejection. Everyone seems to handle his denial differently. (When Dartmouth College rejected me, I turned to both the Dave Matthews Band for enlightenment and Alanis Morrisette for revenge lyrics.) But I do have thoughts about how we can work to normalize college rejection.

Thousands upon thousands of high school students are rejected from at least one college every year. Sharing their (and our) experiences can only help the denial feel *normal*. At one high school, a counselor displayed a "Rejection Wall," where students could opt to publicly hang their college rejection letters. (Seeing the smartest student in European history feel confident about hanging his rejection from Vassar made other rejected students feel better.) At another high school, a beloved history teacher announced his Dartmouth rejection in front of prospective applicants while making small talk with me in the lobby. ("I still cheer on your hockey team, though," he said with a smile.) And at another school, a counselor spoke of his own college rejection as "redirection." (I've always thought it would be incredible for college counselors, teachers, professors, and presidents to hang their own admission and rejection letters in their offices.)

Rejection happens. And in competitive college admissions, *most* are victims of the numbers. But calling a school where one was rejected is likely not going to do much good. Most schools have "decisions are final" policies. Most schools won't share the details of their rejection decisions. Many schools won't have anything to offer a rejected student.

I advise students of rejection to lean on whoever makes them feel better. (The Jonas Brothers might do the trick.) I advise them to talk about their feelings with loved ones. I advise them to grieve if they need to grieve, scream if they need to scream, or feel nothing if they don't feel anything. (Thankfully, not all college rejections hurt and not all students take the rejections hard.) But after the rejection, there's no choice but to move along to an opened gate rather than clinging to one that is closed. (Or, if they are convinced that they belong at a school that rejected them, they can take a gap year* and reapply or eventually apply as a transfer.)

Wait-listed students are a different story. Wait-listed students are still players in the game. Their hats are still in the ring. Their names still could be called. And there are ways to make one's name shine on that list.

At Dartmouth, we wait-listed around one thousand students per year, which was far more than we'd ever need.† It was rare for us to admit more than a few dozen students off the wait list. It was also possible that we wouldn't admit one student after the regular notification. But with such a competitive pool, it was nice to have a wait list option as a kinder way to not admit. (This was the same mentality as casting agents who chose understudies, coaches who had backup pitchers, and heartbreaking mean girls who flirted with their B-team choices. *I'm not going to the prom with you, Johnny, but I promise you'll be my first consideration if Kevin falls sick.*)

Few were "courtesy wait lists," or students put on the wait list because of political reasons. (For example, a college might wait-list a school's strong-but-typical-in-our-pool valedictorian if it admitted a sports recruit ranked thirtieth academically in the same class.) Most were incredibly competitive applicants. They were students who had made it to committee, who had votes to admit from at least one reader, who could have, at

---

* Gap years are nonschool years between high school and university. Popular in Europe and increasingly popular in the United States, they allow students to work, travel, or volunteer before the commitment of college. I've always loved the idea of a gap year (for those who could afford it), since it allows for one more year of maturity, purpose, and direction before returning to the classroom.

† As of 2019, Dartmouth's Undergraduate Admissions "Wait List" website publicly states that "fewer than 10 percent of applicants are offered a place on the wait list."

one point, been sitting in the admit bin. But when we trimmed the fat, when forced to pull students out of the admit bin, when editing the class size, they became victims of the numbers.

Wait list activity was difficult to predict because it had a domino effect. (The pecking order of college choice was clear during wait list season. If Harvard went to the wait list, they would likely pull students from our admitted class. If we went to the wait list, we would likely pull students from Middlebury.) We also didn't rank the wait list. (Why do additional work if there was a decent chance we'd never use the wait list?) We didn't think much about the wait list until forced to do so. (Since the common reply date for most colleges is May 1, we typically wouldn't start plucking from the wait list until mid-May or June.)

Instead, like most colleges, we used the wait list as insurance to steady our profile. If we didn't have enough students from the southwestern United States accept our admissions offer, we'd pluck kids from the wait list from Arizona and New Mexico. If our class was male heavy, we'd take the females. If we needed to raise our average ACT score, those with scores of 32 and above would be in luck.

It was easier for me to predict a roulette number than whether a student would be admitted off the wait list. And my best advice for students was to fall in love with another school. (*"Sorry, Georgetown, but you snooze, you lose. I'm a George Washington University girl now."*) I encouraged students to view their wait list status as a possibility, not as a probability. But if still interested in being admitted, there were steps to take to increase one's probability. If a student was wait-listed, it was important to:

1. Stay "active."
When students are wait-listed, most students are given the option to remain on the wait list or choose to opt out. At Dartmouth, of the thousand or so wait-listed candidates, typically slightly more than half would respond that they remained interested, or "active." We would only choose our admits from those who responded affirmatively to this question.

2. Stay academically engaged.

Often, wait-listed students' final transcripts would be considered in their candidacy. Since we didn't consider many wait-listed students until June, their end-of-the-year results were fair game. If a student wants a chance at admission, he needs to avoid senioritis.

3. Stay squeaky.

Squeaky students got the attention of admissions officers. If we needed humanities majors* in the class, we'd feel more strongly about those who had been in touch postdecision. I advised students (not parents) to clearly make their interest known by e-mail, addressed to the regional admissions officer. Admissions officers aren't looking for desperation (and we certainly didn't need multiple people "touching base" about a student's wait list candidacy), but they are looking for confirmation. And it didn't have to be fancy (or long).

> "While I'm excited by my admission to other universities, School X continues to be my first choice. If admitted, I would be proud to accept an offer in the Class of 2023. Until then, I'll be finishing my senior English thesis on Sandra Cisneros's *The House on Mango Street* (which has captured my heart) and defending home plate as the starting softball catcher in the state playoffs."

Wait-listed students simply needed to show their continued interest and share new information. There was no need to ship cookies to one's regional officer. (This happened occasionally.) There was no need to be *overly* squeaky. (There's a line between the zealous and the overzealous.) And there was no need to visit campus to plead one's case.

---

* Typically, choosing a major didn't matter much (as we knew students would change their minds), unless we went to the wait list. But I advised students to be honest about their intended majors, even if undecided, since betting on "which majors we might need" could be a losing bet.

"There's a wait-listed kid in the lobby who wants to speak with you," the administrative assistant said when she popped her head in my office. "He flew to the U.S. from Tokyo last night."

"Tokyo?"

"That's what he told the receptionist."

"He's probably stopping by on his way to an admitted student event elsewhere. Nobody flies in from Japan just to talk about the wait list."

I was wrong. Jim was a Japanese citizen who attended an international school with a strong English program. He was also a desperate wait-listed student. He came fully armored with a loaded backpack of folders and one of the strongest handshakes I'd encountered.

"Dartmouth is even more beautiful than I imagined." His eyes lit up as he shook my hand vigorously.

We discouraged wait-listed students from visiting campus. We didn't have time for them. We didn't have room for them. (We were busiest in April as both admitted students and rising juniors flocked to campus.) And we didn't have much to offer them. After listening to Jim speak about his (short) time on campus and his interest in the economics department, I knew that I had to go back to my office. "I'm glad you're enjoying the college," I said. "But I'm not sure there is much I can do for you today."

"I know, I know. I just wanted to meet you in person. I don't know what I'll do if I don't get off the wait list."

I'd heard the sentiment before. *I don't know what I'll do. She won't know what she'll do. We won't know what we'll do.* (This one always coming from well-intentioned, yet overinvolved parents.)

Students probably did know. There was likely a plan B, which involved still attending an expensive liberal arts school, still making friends, still majoring in something STEM related. It wasn't plan A. And overachievers were used to plan A.

"Well, I'll keep my fingers crossed for you. I'm sure you'll land on your feet wherever you go," I said with a smile.

Students didn't like this response. It was the equivalent of telling a loved one that there are other fish in the sea. Not being admitted to Dartmouth could potentially be the best thing that could happen to Jim. Maybe he'd go to Syracuse and replace his Big Green sweatshirt with an Orange Crush hoodie. Maybe he'd take a gap year and travel to Honduras, where he'd fall in love with language and become a Spanish translator at the United Nations. Maybe he'd go to a state school, become a vegan, and open a wildly successful on-campus vegetarian sandwich food truck called *Drop Your Pork.*

"There *are* great colleges out there," the student smiled matter-of-factly. "But Dartmouth is where I belong."

Belonging is a funny thing. We can believe we belong somewhere while the universe thinks otherwise. As a Dartmouth admissions director, I met a lot of young people who "knew they belonged at Dartmouth." They had fallen in love with the campus, with the students, with the idea of what college would feel like, be like, smell like, if only they were allowed through the gates. It wasn't bad to love a college. (And it was wonderful to be able to identify a front-runner if applying early.) But it was a bit shortsighted to believe that a student's best college experience could only happen at a singular school. I learned this firsthand as a student, and then as an admissions director.

"Do you mind my asking if you were admitted anywhere else?"

"NYU." He shrugged. "But I'm not that into it."

"Have you been to New York?"

"No. I'm headed there next Monday."

Students had the right to change their minds. Students had the right to not like certain colleges. But they didn't have the right to dislike a college in a city they've never visited. "I think you'll like it. The college takes full advantage of everything the city has to offer."

"Maybe." He shrugged again. "I only applied there because my English teacher is an alum."

"That's not a good reason to apply to a school."

"I only applied here because my math teacher is an alum. But back then I didn't know how perfect Dartmouth is." He handed me a folder filled with documents in protective sleeves. "Here's my updated résumé and a recent research paper. I also included a picture of me onstage as Chip the Teacup in our school's rendition of *Beauty and the Beast*. I was hoping you could add this stuff to my file."

To add the documents, each paper had to be pulled from its sleeve and put through the scanner by a systems technician on the second floor. (The systems tech folks hated staples, three-ring binders, and document sleeves.) The "Chip the Teacup" picture, which was already blurry, would likely look like a pile of black dots after scanning. "Sure," I nodded.

"I also was hoping you could tell me where I stand now on the wait list. Like, what exact number?"

"Oh." I shook my head. "I can't. We don't rank wait-listed students."

"So you can't tell me my chances?"

"No. But I'll certainly put a note in your file that you're very interested." *

"Becky"—my administrative assistant popped her head into the lobby—"a field hockey coach is waiting for you in your office."

"I'm sorry I have to go."

"Yes, yes, of course." He wagged his head like a puppy. "Thank you for your time." He shook my hand vigorously. "I hope we'll be speaking again soon."

I had spent a total of three minutes with the young man. He had traveled nearly six thousand miles. I felt awful but I couldn't offer him anything more than we'd offer any other wait-listed candidate. (We believed that if we started offering any advantages to wait-listed students who visited, we'd attract them all.)

As I walked away, I prayed that he'd find NYU appealing. I hoped that one of the other schools where he was wait-listed would have room for him. I secretly knew he didn't have a chance at Dartmouth. Even in

---

* He would have received the same comment in his file (and saved seven hundred dollars in airplane ticket costs) if he had sent an e-mail stating his interest.

early April, we had already received a significant portion of international student commitments. Of course, I couldn't tell him such.*

We often want what we can't have. In the postdecision, it seemed some students were fixated on the schools that didn't admit them. They seemed more hurt by their rejections than excited by their admissions. They wanted reasons why they weren't admitted into X, even though they didn't seem to care why they were admitted to Y.

My colleagues at other colleges complained of similar sentiments. It seemed that many students were stationed somewhere in the college food chain, and some weren't happy unless they had access to the full buffet.

Students admitted to Colorado College wanted to go to
  Connecticut College.
Students admitted to Connecticut College wanted to go to
  Colorado College.
Students admitted to USC wanted to go to UCLA.
Students admitted to UCLA wanted to go to USC.
There were the Harvard wannabes at Princeton.
And the Princeton wannabees at Harvard.

It never ended. (Except for the unicorn student admitted to all eight Ivies,† which was so rare that the student was whisked to the *Today Show* for the 8:12 a.m. segment with Hoda.)

Yet a rejection letter didn't make a student's accomplishments less relevant, his essay less valid, his recommendations less strong. The business of competitive college admission was built on the rejection majority. And to my knowledge, I never met a rejected Dartmouth applicant who

---

* We didn't comment on the state of the class until the class was finalized. This happened in mid-May, if we didn't go to the wait list, or otherwise later.

† I never understood why a student would *apply* to all eight Ivies, considering the schools are so different from one another. It seemed suspiciously elitist to me.

was not admitted *somewhere*. And usually those *somewheres* were well worth celebrating.

"I'm wondering if you received my additional letter of recommendation from the History Department chair," Kim, a denied student, asked sheepishly over the line.

We had orders from a director never to go back into a file's specific documents. Instead, we were to stick with the summary card. (This way, we wouldn't accidentally blurt information that otherwise shouldn't be shared.) But as with many orders from a director,* I didn't listen. I pulled up Kim's application and snuck a peek. We had her additional letter. We had multiple additional letters. "We did receive the letter, and it was considered with the rest of your application."

"Oh," she said, almost disappointed. "Well, I'm just wondering if there was anything I could have done better."

According to Kim's summary card, there was nothing this woman couldn't do. She was incredibly involved in school and her community. She was yet another competitive applicant who was a superstar that we didn't need in the class. I gave her our canned answer. "It seems that you're an incredibly talented young woman. Unfortunately, we just had a tremendously competitive pool this year."

"I see," she said quietly. "Well, at least I have Colby."

"Colby College?"

"Uh-huh," she said, confused.

"Well then, at *most* you have Colby." I corrected her. "I'm an alumna."

The tone of her voice changed. "Of Colby? In Maine?"

"Yes, ma'am. And let me tell you how lucky you are."

I talked with Kim for nearly a half hour. (I let two other calls go to voice mail.) We laughed about the school mascot (the Mule), we gushed

---

* We were supposed to donate any gift cards we received on the road to the holiday party office raffle. But it was hard to part with a five-dollar Starbucks card (which I received for attending a college fair). I might just have cashed it in for a pumpkin iced latte.

over the English faculty, and we deliberated on which dorm was best for first-year living. Mostly, we cheered her admission.

It felt good to have a conversation with someone about something other than Dartmouth. It was heartening to know students like Kim would populate the next Colby generation. And it was wonderful to celebrate a student's college admission rather than mourning a rejection.

Dartmouth's grass wasn't greener than Colby's. Colby's grass wasn't greener than Dartmouth's. It was all lawn, primed and ready for freshman footsteps. And an invitation to either of these schools (or one of the thousands of others) was an opportunity of a lifetime. It was reason to shout from the rooftops, indulge in the cake, and become excited for one's future. Students could attend only one college. One (affordable) admission was all that was necessary.

"I don't know if this appropriate to say to a Dartmouth admissions officer"—Kim hesitated for a moment—"but I've always liked Colby better. Everyone else was just making a bigger deal over Dartmouth."

"I know," I assured her. "I *know.*"

CHAPTER EIGHTEEN

ADMITTED STUDENT EVENTS

Regular decision admits have limited time to choose the college they'll attend. Most students are notified of their admission in late March and must complete their "intent to enroll" forms by May 1. The month of April is one of the most frantic for college-bound students as they hustle to visit colleges, compare tuition costs, and make an ultimate decision.

I spent most of April smiling at people. I smiled while making small talk with mothers of admitted students who were (still) wondering about the winters. I smiled while handing out luggage tags to visiting students who needed a place to store their bags. I smiled while circling campus to round up any lost visitors (who couldn't locate the dessert reception for students interested in the humanities). And I smiled while trying to answer students' last-minute questions, regardless of how obscure.

"I'm assuming I can bring Jaws to campus, right?"

Carla was an admitted senior from Oregon who had taken a red-eye flight to Dartmouth for our admitted student program. While we waited for her overnight host at campus registration, I made small talk. "Jaws?" I asked.

"My goldfish," she responded matter-of-factly. "I want to make sure he's allowed in my dorm room."

I had no idea if the college allowed fish. But I wasn't about to take the time to ask. "I can't imagine goldfish aren't allowed."

"Great." Carla smiled. "Some of the other schools I'm considering don't allow fish tanks in dorms."

Firstly, I wondered if Dartmouth didn't allow goldfish, considering we'd likely have similar pet policies to the other institutions. Secondly, I couldn't imagine the ability to bring a goldfish would be a reason to choose one college over another. "If it's that important, maybe you should double-check with residential life," I suggested.

"No, it's cool. I trust you," she said. "You seem much more knowledgeable than anyone I met during my other college visits last week."

I wasn't to be trusted. Sure, I was knowledgeable about the college *in general*. I was an expert on the majors we offered. I was an expert on the options for student life. But I'd never been an undergraduate* student at Dartmouth. I'd never been on a Dartmouth Outing Club trip, to a sorority party, or to an infamous language drill class. I'd only stepped foot in a Dartmouth undergraduate dorm room once (to visit my much younger sister-in-law), and I had no idea if students kept goldfish as pets. "Well, let me know if you have other questions."

"Actually, I do," Carla continued. "The truth is I'm leaning toward Boston University. I mean, I grew up in rural Oregon, so this is my one chance to be in a city. But I really love Dartmouth's commitment to undergraduate teaching and the small size of the English classes. Where do you think I should go?"

I had met Carla four minutes earlier. I didn't know anything about her other than her amazing ability to name goldfish. I had no idea where she should spend four years of college. "You should go to the school that makes the most sense."

"Aren't you supposed to tell me I should go to Dartmouth?"

"Only if Dartmouth makes the most sense."

She looked at me with a frown. Apparently, I wasn't as knowledgeable as she'd hoped. "I mean, yeah, Dartmouth makes sense. But so does BU. They both make sense in different ways."

---

* As a two-year graduate student in Dartmouth's master of arts in liberal studies program, I lived on campus in graduate student dorms. I had experience as a Dartmouth *graduate* student (who never used the undergraduate dining halls, the gym, or the student center) but none as an undergraduate.

"Then consider yourself lucky." I smiled. "If they both make sense, either will work out."

It was my honest answer. After students were admitted to Dartmouth, I was happy to answer their questions about the college. I would try to convince them that Dartmouth was a good place to spend four years. But I wasn't going to argue that it was a better experience than another college. It wasn't my place to fight for one over another. It was only my place to celebrate Dartmouth's offerings. Their decisions were their own.

There are multiple individual considerations when choosing a college. I've met students who have made their college matriculation decisions based predominately on:

Job security
Net price
Ability to play a sport
Proximity to loved ones
The college's support for students of X background
Diploma prestige

The decision is personal. And while I've been surprised by students' ultimate college decisions (including the woman from Palo Alto who did literal backflips for Dartmouth but turned down our offer), I've never walked in their shoes. Some had understandable reasons. (Student debt seemed to me to be incredibly important when considering an institution.) Some had reasons I would never understand. (One student chose another Ivy League institution over Dartmouth to avoid "all the flannel.") And a few, like me, had reasons a student would be embarrassed to admit.

I chose to matriculate at Colby because of its all-male "Mr. Colby" pageant. My decision wasn't based on financial aid packages (which were similar), the faculty (who were equally accomplished and accessible), the curriculums (strong English majors were offered at all schools), or the campuses (all boasted well-maintained grass). Instead, I chose Colby because the pageant was hysterical,* the community was supportive, and the student body seemed happy. I *liked* happy.

My other college visits varied. I spent one campus visit at a school filled with friends I already knew, buildings I'd already visited, and coaches I already trusted. At another, I marveled at the friendliness of their faculty. But at College Z, I was paired with a sophomore who wasn't thrilled with her experience. I spent the visit in her off-campus apartment, listening to her cigarette-addicted boyfriend ramble on about indie rock. Neither of them seemed to be very invested or interested in what was happening on campus.

Colby was a good decision (regardless of how I made it). But senior year, I spent most of my college weekends with a boyfriend who attended College Z. He lived off campus only a few blocks away from where I had spent my miserable prospective student evening. I'd quickly learn that College Z was a pretty similar school to Colby. I had fun attending their college traditions. I was impressed by the intellect and engagement of the student body. And I realized that I had just been unlucky those years ago when I was paired with an indifferent student.

What I learned from this experience is that I likely would have been engaged, challenged, and motivated at any of these schools. Most students would similarly learn, grow, and spread their wings at more than one institution. Yet they can choose only one. Sometimes the decision is based on family needs. (In Miami, I met a young man who chose to stay in state over attending Dartmouth because he didn't want to abandon his single mother.) Sometimes the decision is based on financial needs. (In New Jersey, a father from a low-income household took on a third job to

---

* The winner chain-sawed a stool from a log, then proceeded to sit down on it and chug a beer.

make his daughter's first-choice college payments. "She won't appreciate it until she's a parent herself," he had said to me.) Sometimes the decision is based on personal preferences. (In Salt Lake City, one young woman chose to turn down our offer after an unlikable peer matriculated.) And sometimes, as in my case, the decision is based on a little luck.

Admissions officers knew we couldn't compete with luck. But we could do our best to compete with other colleges. During the month of April, we'd bend over backward to win over our admitted students. And we'd start by inviting them to campus.

On-campus yield events were choreographed admitted student visitation programs. During these days, we'd convince our most articulate and charming college colleagues to offer special lectures, open-house programs, and community receptions. We'd distribute perks to visiting families, including campus gym passes, coupons to the bookstore, and "Dartmouth" Nalgene water bottles. And we'd offer free transportation (including planes, trains, and bus rides) to students who qualified financially.

These campus events required cooperation from college partners. Our professors welcomed prospectives into their classes, our dining hall offered a few more pizza toppings, and our student groups organized a few more campus events than usual. During these visit days, the grass was always green, the food was always at its best, and the parking tickets were more forgiving. (I was involved with at least two forgiven tickets.)

Whether or not a student attended an on-campus yield event, he might also be invited to an off-campus admitted student reception. These events were localized opportunities for alumni to connect with prospective students. (Much like with alumni interviews, we capitalized on our alumni's willingness to assist recruitment efforts.) Typically, an off-campus reception was thrown at the (impeccable) home of an active alumni interviewer. Dartmouth held dozens of these events annually, inviting alumni and admitted students to schmooze over expensive cheeses and nonalcoholic drinks. At any event, there were typically a few older gentlemen in Dartmouth ties (waxing nostalgic about their fraternity days), midcareer alumni (in expensive shoes), and chatty young alumni (overeager to give dining hall recommendations).

On-campus yield events could be overwhelming. (Spending the night in a campus dorm with a stranger was not every student's first choice.) Off-campus yield events could be obnoxious. (The opulence of the host homes could be intimidating, despite the host's good intentions.) But they were the best our offices could do to help students make their ultimate decisions.

At this point in the process, the ball was in the student's court. The admitted student, ultimately, had the power to accept or deny our admissions decision. Before the student made a final college choice, I urged her to use this power to her benefit. There were three specific things a student could do.

1. Speak up.

Perhaps a student was mismatched with her overnight host. Perhaps an economics professor was less than dynamic. Perhaps an alumna in Detroit spoke more about her frat party attendance than her forensics major.

It happens. But no admissions office wanted a student to have a singular campus experience or listen to a singular alumna's opinion. We'd do what we could to rectify a negative experience *if a student brought it to our attention.* We'd happily connect a student (in person or otherwise) with other college community members to hear various perspectives. We'd refigure a student's visit so he could audit another econ class. We'd take alternative measures to ensure a student's multidimensional understanding of campus. (We didn't want to sugarcoat a college experience, but we also didn't want one bad apple spoiling the bunch.)

2. Appeal a financial aid award, if relevant.

Most colleges and universities are happy to take a second look at a financial aid award. Also, some colleges will match financial aid awards from other institutions. (For example, Dartmouth would match need-based awards from a select group of competitor schools.) It's always worth asking the financial aid office to reconsider before finalizing one's decision.

3. Ask for an "intent to enroll" extension, if there is (good) reason.

A little-known secret of college admissions is that we'd happily grant extensions to admitted students in need. We'd give extensions to students who were awaiting financial aid appeals, students who couldn't visit campus until (slightly) after the deadline, students who were dealing with personal hardship, and so on. We had (some) flexibility around our May 1 deadline. A student just needed to ask.

Our admissions office wasn't at the mercy of our admitted students. (Lord knows, we had plenty of students waiting for their spots on the wait list.) But we did want the students we chose to come. (Ego certainly came into play when a class was perfectly yielded. Denial came into play when a class was underenrolled. Dread came into play when a class was overenrolled.)* We wanted students to utilize Dartmouth's resources. We wanted students to be productive and *happy*. And we desperately wanted to move on to the next year's class.

Dartmouth was going to be a tremendous opportunity for an admitted student. As was the University of Wisconsin–Madison. And Gonzaga, Northeastern, and Dallas Baptist University. If a student did his homework during the application process, he probably couldn't make a bad decision.

Still, I met hundreds of admitted college students who struggled with this choice. What should have felt celebratory sometimes felt stressful, particularly when financial aid was involved. After a grueling admissions

---

* There were years when the college was unsure where its overenrolled class members were going to sleep. The housing office would scramble to figure out alternative arrangements. In 2001, Dartmouth offered a year of free housing to students who agreed to defer one year.

process, choosing the "right" college often felt even more critical for these young people. (One memorable young lady told me that making the decision felt "paralyzing.")

But there is no *one* "right" college. There are many. And for the privileged students who had multiple offers of admission, the best advice was also the simplest:

Choose one. Move forward. And make it count.

CHAPTER NINETEEN

WELCOME TO COLLEGE

Most girls at the middle school cheerleading tryouts could perform a back handspring. I could barely cartwheel. But I made up for my lack of flexibility with overzealous enthusiasm. I flashed big smiles. I hollered big cheers. I gestured big, purposeful head nods as my ponytail waved in the sky. I gave the tryout my best, knowing that, at most, I might make the junior varsity team.

When they called my name for *varsity*, my jaw dropped. (As did all the other jaws in the room.) I was one of a few seventh graders on a team of mostly eighth-grade, back-handspring experts. I had been chosen. And within seconds, my ego grew taller than my high ponytail.

Clearly, I was better than I had originally believed. Obviously, I was more special than the other wannabes in the gymnasium. Undoubtedly, I had the golden touch.

I walked into the first day of practice with my head held high and my confidence soaring. But within the first hour, the reason I was chosen for the varsity team became apparent. I was a big girl. A strong girl. A girl much larger and broader and wider than anyone else on the team. When it was time for the others to form their pyramids, they needed a base. I was perfect for the position.

Being the base of the pyramid was not what I had envisioned. I was grounded while the other girls flew high in the sky. I was bruised and bumped as fellow cheerleaders used me as a ladder. I was stuck in the back row, waiting for "formation" as others hopped toward the front row, ponytails waving.

But I kept swinging my ponytail. I made friends with the girls I'd toss to the sky. I grew more synchronized, more graceful, more confident.

And I learned how to be a better cheerleader, which is all I'd hoped for in the first place.

I learned a very important lesson during my (short-lived) cheerleading days. Sometimes you'll be chosen. Other times you won't. Often the choice will be for unknown reasons.* But being chosen doesn't mean you're *better* than anyone else. It doesn't mean you're worse. It just means that you were the right person at the right time, and you'd best make the most of the opportunity.

I'd reflect on my cheerleading days every September as first-year students were dropped off for their optional (but not really optional)† orientation trips. On the sidewalk next to the arriving students, *Welcome Home* was written in chalk. It was a nice sentiment. A nod to a student's sense of community as she embarked on four years in a tiny New Hampshire town. But we all knew Dartmouth would never really be home. Home was the place they'd call when they were homesick. Home was the place where their little sister took over the top bunk. Home was the place where the chicken parmigiana tasted exactly as it should.

College, on the other hand, was more of a four-year stopover. For most, it was a darn wonderful stopover with bountiful private libraries, dorm air-conditioning, and golf course access. It was a time of privilege and resources. (The sidewalk should have read, *Welcome to an Expensive Temporary Housing Situation with Fabulous Froyo.*) And it was an opportunity for students to become smarter, better, and more prepared for our world.

---

* After bumping into Scarlett Johansson at a restaurant, my husband (then single) asked her on a date. "She had to say yes to someone," he argued. It wasn't his turn, apparently.

† If a student chose not to participate, he'd receive a phone call from an upperclassman, encouraging his attendance.

I watched the first-year students from my corner office window as they awkwardly made introductions to one another. They were young, anxious, and seemingly intimidated by the wildly colorful upperclassman dancing to the latest pop music. They reminded me of myself as a first-year student:* unsure, self-aware, and eager to laugh at anything an upperclassman uttered.

These students were the varsity cheerleaders. They were the chosen ones. They were selected from thousands of other applicants for various reasons and talents. They were the folks who would fill our chemistry labs and row our boats and eat our gnocchi. They were Brooke from Philadelphia and Karlos from Santa Ana and Mallory from Key West. They were talented, accomplished, bright, and funny. They were *it*.

But as an admissions officer who selected them from a pool of incredible applicants, I knew that they weren't necessarily *better* than anyone who was denied. They were just good business decisions.

"She's so excited," Caroline's mother said to me as she swung by the admissions office after dropping off her daughter. "So far, Dartmouth is everything she's dreamed."

Caroline was admitted by the skin of her teeth after a tortuous admissions committee. Her mother had no idea how close she came to the wait list. But it didn't matter how she was admitted. Caroline had made the cut.

"I'm glad she's enjoying it," I said.

"She really is, Becky," the mother gushed. "I want to thank you for everything you've done. We're very grateful."

---

* I spent the night before I was dropped off at college in the bathroom of a Holiday Inn. It was the day Princess Diana had died. My parents were glued to the television. My sister was glued to her comic books. And I was glued to the bathroom floor. I was incredibly nervous. But the second I climbed the stairs to my dorm room and was greeted by smiley roommates who offered to carry in my mini fridge, I knew I'd be okay.

In the history of my career, I'd only been thanked by a dozen admitted students.* I didn't need their thanks, especially since I wasn't alone in making admissions decisions. But it felt nice to be acknowledged. "I'm just happy she found a college that makes her happy."

"And we're just happy you recognized Caroline's potential. She's just so deserving."

I'd read Caroline's application and served on her admissions committee. Caroline had worked her tail off in high school. She'd spent hours perfecting the clarinet, rose to the top of her class, and followed school rules. She'd put in the work. She was an amazing young lady both on paper and in person. (I met Caroline and her mother while they were at an off-campus information session.) But I wasn't convinced she was more "deserving" than other candidates.

I never liked the word "deserving" when it came to college admissions. Admissions officers weren't in the business of choosing who was most deserving. We were in the business of choosing a class. Our choices were a reflection of what Dartmouth wanted to be (tangibly more academic competitive), who Dartmouth wanted to educate (young people of diverse backgrounds), and what Dartmouth was (a liberal arts university, trying to appease the alumni and student body while also remaining fiscally sound). Our selections were not based on worthiness. Our selections were based on the college's growth.

I understood the mother's sentiment, however. Caroline was a member of one of the most impossibly selective clubs in the country. She'd be surrounded by classmates handpicked to be her peers. There was Debbie, the straight-A student and starting basketball center who received the very first "likely" letter of the class. There was Tate, who was cited by his teachers as the most brilliant math mind on the reservation. There was Teddy, the billionaire's son who thrived at five different international

---

* Interestingly, in my entire career, I was invited to only one college graduation party. But I received plenty of invites to high school seniors' senior plays before they were admitted.

high schools in four years as his family constantly relocated. They'd share a special bond as classmates and alumni. And as a class, their strengths, accomplishments, and accolades were many.

From where I sat, I knew that each student (even the billionaire's son) was talented. What they would bring to Dartmouth wouldn't have changed if they went elsewhere. A valedictorian was no less intellectual if he was not admitted to Dartmouth. A soccer player's footwork wasn't faster if she was recruited by Marquette. No interesting, intellectual, incredible young person was any *more* or *less* because of the school they were or were not attending. They were still themselves, chock-full of strengths, weaknesses, and everything in between.

I hoped students would celebrate their college picks. After they were admitted and selected a college, I wanted them to party. I wanted them to throw a family brunch with Mom's famous peach and mint salad, Dad's infamous home fries, and sister Sasha's not-yet-famous-but-bound-to-be "Dartmouth Green Eggs and Ham." I wanted them to wear their Dartmouth sweatshirts until holes formed in the armpits. I wanted them to squeal at the thought of learning from the professor who wrote the book. I wanted them to be proud of their hard work and excited for their future.

But I also wanted them to recognize the investment made by the college. As an admissions officer, I knew how equally special the students were who were rejected from Dartmouth.* I knew the poetry talent of the denied and the extracurricular talents of those who never escaped the wait list. I had done the sorting. I knew what was lost. And I knew every investment we made in a student was an investment we couldn't make in another.

Obviously, the student was making an investment in his education as well. There was no time to slack off, act like a nincompoop, or waste a moment. (I sadly witnessed the decline of a few students who couldn't

---

* I once made a speech welcoming international students to campus as "the best and brightest." Now I regret my choice of words.

pull their acts together after arriving on campus. Alcohol and peer pressure contributed to their downfalls.) The college had limited tolerance for students who didn't take an active part in their own learning. (A friend who worked in the tutoring center was excited to help those in need but unable to force a student to ask for help.) And there was no respect for the student who bragged about his place at the school. (At the campus coffee shop, I once heard a Dartmouth student brag to another that he was admitted in a more competitive pool as a "white male." The other student, who was a white female, quickly responded, "They needed to fill the asshole quota." I laughed so hard my latte came through my nostrils.)

"I'm unsure if I really want to major in economics," Christopher said as he fiddled with a grape tootsie roll pop in my office. "It doesn't matter if I change what I put on my application, right?"

It didn't matter. Students didn't proclaim their majors until sophomore year. (Undecided was one of the top incoming majors at the college.) "Not at all."

"And if I end up not playing frisbee, that's cool, too, right? You guys aren't going to be mad or anything."

I didn't care if he played frisbee or leapfrog. "We would never be mad."

"And I know that I mentioned that I wanted to start a K-pop radio station, but I'm not sure if that makes sense now."

I stared at Christopher. He was a lanky kid, with a tear in his jeans and glasses propped on his forehead. I'd met him at a high school visit in Georgia before he was admitted early decision. He was an outlier in the freshman class with the confidence of an upperclassman. But his honesty was starting to make me wonder. "You're not forced to do anything you wrote on your application. But you should really be doing something."

"Yeah, yeah, I know, I know." He nodded. "I'm going to do lots of things. I just want to focus on classes before I commit to any one thing."

It was a good argument. First-year college students had a lot to learn. Academics came first, followed by clubs, organizations, and hullaballoo. "Fair enough." I leaned back in my chair. "But promise me that you won't wait until spring semester to visit the art museum."

"Why the art museum?" He laughed. "I'm not really into art."

"Doesn't matter." I smiled at him. "It's there and you're here."

I didn't care if Christopher ever joined the frisbee team. I knew for a fact that playing frisbee wasn't a ploy to be more competitive in the college admissions process. (I trusted Christopher's counselor, who vouched for his authenticity of interests.) I also knew that even if he wanted to start a K-pop radio station on campus, there might not be room for new programming. (Memberships in activities on campus were usually more selective than high school clubs. Not everyone who debated in high school was going to have the opportunity to debate in college.)

But I also knew that the art museum on campus was free for students. I knew that it cost nothing to attend the visiting lecture by Dr. Cornel West. And I knew there was only one chance to run around the bonfire at homecoming.*

College is a big transition for students. A university classroom would be filled with confident, articulate, and intellectual voices. Students with less preparation would have to dig deep to thrive. (Many colleges offer mentoring programs for first-generation students.) Every first-year student, no matter how prepared, would slowly learn the ropes of classes without bells, professors with limited office hours, lectures without blackboards.

But there was always time to maximize opportunity, especially since college employees were working so hard for these youngsters. I had friends who spent their days making college more exciting, more interesting, and more accessible for underclassmen. One friend worked

---

* Running around the homecoming bonfire was a first-year tradition. As *Lord of the Flies* as it sounds, it was exciting to witness.

the early shift at the dining hall, making sure the omelets were piping hot and full of diverse veggie options. A friend who was a physical trainer arrived at the fitness center at six in the morning, bright-eyed, bushy-tailed and appropriately caffeinated to make sure the equipment was ready for morning runners. A friend who taught first-year students beamed about his preference for underclassmen who hadn't yet been tainted by the pressures to "score big-name internships."

I wanted students to have fun. But I also wanted them to go to every class.* I wanted them to join the clubs, kick the balls, do the things. I wanted them to visit the organic farm because they could. I wanted them to stop worrying about checked boxes and start worrying about missed opportunities. (Ahem, build the snow sculpture, kiddos.)

Mostly, I wanted them to recognize college as a privilege, not a right. No matter the ranking of the school, no matter the color of the sweatshirt, no matter the location, colleges were working hard to offer a student the chance to *grow*. The investment in these young people was not to be wasted.

"Join us in celebrating the college decisions of the students of Huckleberry High School," the card read. "Thank you for your help in ensuring bright futures for our young people." The photo featured about thirty young men and women wearing various college T-shirts. Lafayette. Rutgers. University of Miami. County College of Morris. Montclair State. UVA. NYU. Dartmouth. New Jersey Institute of Technology. Vanderbilt. James Madison. Franklin & Marshall. Rowan University. Pitt.

I'd received the photo in an e-mail from a school counselor who

---

* My husband missed only one class during his four years at Dartmouth (to attend his grandmother's funeral). By his math, each class cost approximately three hundred dollars. As a student on financial aid, he wasn't going to squander that investment. He went to classes hungover, sick, and half asleep. But he always got his bum in a seat.

wanted to thank admissions officers for their help in selecting students from their school. I usually spent about three seconds on this sort of e-mail. But on that June day, I lingered on the picture. It was colorful. It was interesting. It was a distraction from my real work.

The students in the picture were as diverse as their college shirts. (I was confident that this was only a sampling of the senior class. I was sure that a few of their classmates weren't heading to college for various reasons.) Their arms were placed around each other, showing unity. The photograph wasn't perfect, as the student in the NYU shirt wasn't looking in the direction of the camera, and the James Madison student was caught speaking midword. But all were smiling. All looked excited for their futures. All looked young and full of promise.

The student in the Vanderbilt shirt looked no happier than the student in the Montclair State shirt. The student in the private college shirt looked no happier than the student in the community college shirt. The student in the blue shirt looked no happier than the student in the green shirt. Each looked proud of his uniform. Each looked good in his uniform. Each looked thrilled.

These students would likely receive a lot of advice before embarking on their college journeys. Friends, family, teachers, and mentors would surely have plenty of suggestions. "Show up to office hours." "Get some sleep." "Call your mom." I'd heard folks give a lot of this advice. (The convocation speeches were filled with the dean's lofty aspirations for the new classes.) And I, too, could give a list worth of suggestions, some more specific than others. ("Claim the bed nearest the window." "Write your name on the tag of your winter coat." "Don't skip the shower shoes." "Stop using the word 'stuff' in academic papers.")

But my most important advice for a first-year was to make a return on the investment. The college's admissions office had made an investment with each admit. Families had made an investment with their tuition dollars. And individuals had made an investment with their own time, energy, and choices. This was the time . . .

To learn from people with differing opinions. (Admissions officers create diverse classes for the purpose of learning from each
other. Some of the most memorable college conversations tend to
happen after hours, among friends, involving pizza.)

To swim, try the quinoa, and spin some pottery. (College students
have a breadth of resources that likely will be unmatched for the
remainder of their lives.)

To seek out mentors and mentorships. (College campuses are
chock-full of people who love to teach, to instruct, to coach. A
student needed to capitalize on these human resources.)

And to step up, stand up, and raise a hand because one's name
was called.

At the end of the first term, Christopher returned to my office. He
had joined the frisbee team. He had tried out (and was cast) for a small
role in the fall musical. He had done well in his first-term classes. And he
had visited the art museum.

Over the next four years, he left few stones unturned. He completed
his computer science major and picked up a minor in Spanish while studying in Barcelona. He joined a fraternity, made regular use of the multimedia lab, took salsa lessons, and learned how to snowboard. He toured the
Daniel Webster library, kayaked up the Connecticut River, and inspired
a friend to join him in an overnight camping trip. He dabbled, sam-
pled, and tinkered his way through campus, all while balancing his
time for academics. And when he graduated, he was more interesting,
more open-minded, and more experienced.* He had made the most of

---

* After graduation, we kept in touch. Christopher's position as a lab technician in
a northeastern suburb didn't offer many extracurricular perks. He had no time or
money for a gym membership. There were no community options for kayaking,

Dartmouth's many opportunities, which in turn had helped make the most of his person.

When I look back at my own college experience, I have regrets. I wish I'd had the courage to try out for the improv group. I wish I'd developed more lasting relationships with professors. I wish I'd discovered those hidden cross-country ski trails long before senior year. I wish *I had* gone to the art museum. (I never stepped foot in the Colby art museum until I attended a reunion as an alumna of the college.)

My college experience is history. But the smiling students in the card from Huckleberry High are just beginning their adventures. The students on the Dartmouth quad are just arriving to their new "home." Caroline from Pittsburgh is just showing up to the college she worked hard to attend.

These folks may or may not be more deserving than others. They may or may not be more brilliant. But their names have been called. Their uniforms have been pressed. They've made the varsity team.

Now, it's showtime.

---

farming, or intramural kickball. And while he did find a local frisbee league, he found himself missing the days of discs on the quad.

CHAPTER TWENTY

BEST IN CLASS

As I went into labor at Dartmouth-Hitchcock Medical Center, I was *still* talking college. My obstetrician's son went to Colby, my alma mater. So did the nurse who stood at my side, checking my vitals. We made the connection sometime between my screaming and their doctoring. As I huffed and puffed, it seemed that even in life's biggest moments I couldn't escape college chitchat. But in this case the distraction was welcome.

On a drizzling September evening, Rudy was born. He had a strong heartbeat, a full head of thick, black hair, and a scream heard through the maternity ward. He was healthy, he was handsome, he was loved.

When the news broke, I received warm wishes from friends, family, and loved ones. My voice mail gurgled with shrieks from girlfriends. My mailbox overflowed with cards from overzealous aunts. And an admissions colleague bragged that my son's timely arrival (being born on his due date) put him in the top 5 percent of all infants nationwide. Statistically, he was already a standout. But I knew better. A person was much more than his numbers.

I left my position at Dartmouth a few months after Rudy was born.*

---

* On the day I packed up my office, I found a small granite peg, thoughtfully gifted to me from the admissions dean who denied me, and then hired me, many years ago. A meaningful and odd gift, it had been drilled from the steps of the admissions building, as constructed crews installed a new steel handrail. It was meant as a memento of community, allowing me to physically own a piece of Dartmouth's history. But for me, it was something more. It was a reminder that I was responsible for those walking both up and down those steps, those who would come and those who would

(I stayed on through the reading season as a part-time employee, then left permanently at the end of March.) Choosing to leave the admissions office was difficult. I missed the paycheck, surely. But I also missed my colleagues (and our eyerolls at personal statements about "The Lessons Learned on Family Yachting Trip to Mallorca"). I missed the travel. ('Til we meet again, Swaziland.) I missed my office. (I did not miss the bitter office coffee, the in-swinging bathroom door, or the hunt for decent parking.) And I sorely missed reading applications, a task that had become one of my favorite parts of the job.

But being outside the admissions office was freeing. I could speak to families about other college choices. I could listen, *really* listen, to their honest concerns about the process. (If a student complained to me about legacy admissions when I worked at the college, I'd brush them off and say I couldn't comment.) I could share my own defenses and criticisms of college access. But most of all, I could share my perspective as the chooser of the chosen.

I knew I wasn't alone in my longing for decency in the college admissions process. (My *New York Times* op-ed about the janitor recommendation confirmed my belief. The piece garnered over four hundred online comments, dozens of e-mails, and one heartfelt anonymous letter from an immigrant parent who noted she was touched "in ways you cannot imagine.") The process has become one of the most complicated hurdles of the American education system, and students were doing "whatever it takes" to edge out the competition. They were checking boxes. They were sharpening their elbows. Everyone was trying to be the most impressive candidate admitted to the most impressive institution.

But perhaps they needed to reassess their definition of "impressiveness." Perhaps they needed to realize how many wonderful colleges and universities exist in the United States. Perhaps they needed to hear an

---

go. I cherished the peg throughout my career, and it still sits on my at-home desk, reminding me of my time in McNutt Hall.

admissions officer's take on the ones who got away. Perhaps they needed some perspective.

As I stood in the parking lot of the rented reception hall, I pulled my raincoat hood up over my head. The valedictorians were circling. I didn't want them to notice me. I was tired of their efforts to impress.

These prospective students were lovely young people. But our conversations had felt like auditions, rather than engagements. Everyone had been the cleverest, the brightest, the most accomplished. They handed me résumés chock-full of superlatives and accolades. But my feet hurt from cheap heels, my face hurt from a four-hour perma-smile, and my stomach ached from hunger. (Although the buffet spread at the admissions events was bountiful, I was so busy talking to parents that not one crab cake crossed my lips.) I needed my car. And I needed it fast.

Unfortunately, I had committed a rookie mistake of valet parking. (As an admissions director with years of experience at these sorts of events, I should have known better. When I arrived, I had so many boxes of brochures, name tags, and green-and-white alumni swag, I conceded to the valet.) Now, standing in the misty and foggy remains of a recent thunderstorm, I was at the mercy of waiting for the attendant. There was nothing to do but stand still and hope families wouldn't bother me with additional questions about Dartmouth. I watched them carefully and eavesdropped on their conversations as they walked past me on the pavement.

"I think I better stick with swimming so that I have a sport on my résumé," a son muttered to his dad.

"Did you notice she didn't mention the frats?" one daughter mentioned to her mother.

"They sure are spending our good money on politically correct crap," an alumnus muttered to his wife.

They paraded to the lot, mumbling to each other about this and that, most likely saving their juiciest comments for the privacy of the car.

They carried Dartmouth brochures, to-go brownies, and heavy sets of car keys.

"Can I help you, ma'am?" The valet approached from the lot. He was a thin-framed teenager who didn't look old enough to drive, never mind handle valet parking. His baggy uniform jacket hung from his shoulders as if he was wearing his father's coat.

I handed him my valet ticket. "It's a Toyota with New Hampshire plates."

"Be right up!" The valet walked swiftly, nearly catching up to the family of the swimmer.

On the foggy pavement, a frog had appeared in the path of the families and the valet. The others had seemingly seen and stepped around it. The valet stopped in his tracks. He squatted to the ground and cupped the frog with his hands. He walked it to the edge of the lot and released it at the outskirts of the woods.

Under a minute later, he arrived with my car. "Anything else I can help you with?" He stepped out of the driver's seat.

"I'm all set." I handed him a five-dollar bill as I sat down in the driver's seat. Then I looked back at the valet. "I saw what you did with the frog."

The valet looked ashamed. "I hope I didn't take too long. I just didn't want the little guy becoming squished by someone not paying attention."

"No, no, I didn't mind." I smiled and paused for a second. "In fact, I was really impressed. Nobody else stopped for the poor creature."

"One of those girls nearly stomped it with her heel," he said. "I'm sure she had more important things on her mind than watching her step." He shrugged. "I heard this was an *Ivy League* event."

I couldn't help but chuckle. (The valet attendant was obviously confused by my laughter.) "I'm Becky," I said as I outstretched my hand.

"Ernie," the valet said as he shook my hand. "Probably should have washed the frog slime from my hands before shaking with you."

"No bother." I reached deep into my front blazer pocket. "You know, I'm not sure if you have higher education plans, but I'm an admissions officer at Dartmouth. If you were ever interested in checking out the college or just generally talking about college admissions in general, I'd be happy to chat with you." I handed over one of my business cards.

"Dartmouth?" he asked earnestly as he read the card. "It's in New Hampshire, right?"

I nodded.

He looked at the card again. "And it's a really good school, right?"

"People think so."

"And you're the one who makes the decisions?"

"I'm one-third of the vote."

"Sheesh," he smiled. "That must be a hard job . . . especially with kids like those." He nodded toward the parking lot. "They're pretty impressive."

I shrugged. "None of *them* took the time to save the frog."

"It was no biggie." He shut the door behind me as he blushed. "Drive safely, ma'am, and thanks again."

I rolled down the window. "Thank *you.*"

Chances were Ernie was not going to be admitted to Dartmouth. Chances were that every other student at the prospective student event was not going to be admitted either. The odds were against everyone in the Dartmouth admissions pool.

Saving a frog wasn't something for a résumé. But it was a breath of fresh air. At that event and beyond, our kids were turning into laser-focused robots for a chance at the college dream. To stand out even among the extraordinary, applicants were going beyond the call of duty. If we told them to do community service, they would book flights to underserved countries. If we told them to take AP French, they'd become Camembert cheese experts. If we told them to stick four stuffed mushrooms in their mouth at one time, they'd find a way to squeeze in five. Meanwhile, many were blinded to the world around them, to the opportunities that didn't "count," to the frog.

As a director, I was a witness and accomplice to the craziness of the college admissions process. I sympathized with students in the game. The process was less than transparent. There was plenty of bad advice to be shared. The playing field was unequal. And we kept increasing the number of hoops that they needed to jump through.

I don't have all the answers on how to stop the madness. But I do have some suggestions for colleges across the country. I'd like to invite other people with relevant perspectives on candidacies to the selection table. (I've always admired schools that invite professors to sit on their committees.) I'd like "counselor calls" to stop. I'd like for legacy to not matter in the process. (Preference in legacy review never sat right with me, particularly because of the lack of legacy diversity in many pools.) I'd like colleges with ridiculously low acceptance rates to stop recruiting overrepresented populations. (There was no reason to travel to predominantly white, wealthy high schools in suburban Illinois just to rally more applications. If we wanted a more talented and diverse class, we needed to shift our recruitment, not repeat it). And I'd like media outlets to stop publishing rank. (Slim chance, but a girl can dream.)

Of course, I can do my part in slowing the madness. I can tell my stories. I can assure a student that an admissions officer prefers a handful of meaningful extracurricular activities to a laundry list. I can assure folks that very accomplished and inspiring young people were denied from Dartmouth simply because we didn't have enough room. I can help students identify colleges off the beaten path, assuring them that the Ivy isn't always greener. (There's no need to turn into an Ivy clinger when there are thousands of wonderful colleges and universities in the United States.) And I can vouch that the most impressive young people I met hung their hats on their decency, not on the brand names of their diplomas.

Students can do their part as well. They can concentrate on best *preparing* themselves for college, not best positioning themselves. They can use the application process as an exercise in self-advocacy. They can be as thoughtful about supplemental essays as they are the personal statement because they take pride in *all* work. And they can preserve their dignity by recognizing that colleges' ultimate decisions are judgments of applications, not people.

The further I move from the process, the more perspective I gain on the work. Colleges don't admit "the best" students. They admit the applicants who are best for them. Despite admissions officers' thoughtful work, at the end of the day, they are conducting business. No Dartmouth admit had bragging rights over a Dartmouth deny. No wait-listed student was any more impressive than the student who was outright rejected. No rejected student was any less qualified for a college because of his denial letter from the college.

Today, I'm the mother of two toddlers. (My second child, Polly, was born twenty-two months after her older brother.) In some ways, one would think that being an admissions director would prepare me for being a mother. I am a human encyclopedia on applicants to the Ivy League. I spent my life around academic young people. I have read countless essays about the meaningful life experiences of kids. I know which schools produce the greatest percentage of college-bound students. I have witnessed the pitfalls of pushing a kid too early to be a soccer star and the regrets of students who never bothered to learn a language. I know how to help my children best angle their college applications.

But as I learned over the years in my profession, attending elite universities doesn't necessarily make students impressive *people*. While I want my children to have every opportunity for higher learning, I care more about decency than Ivy. While I hope they go to college, I can honestly say that I'd be happy if they continue to open books, ask questions, and be productive members of society.

As I imagine a future for my children, the definition of "success" starts to blur. After my experience in competitive college admissions, I've learned that a student's character is more important than the college decal on his car. (Anyone can buy a Harvard sweatshirt, after all.) I want to raise a kid who stands out for the right reasons. The kid who cares more about kindness than clout. The kid who is more sympathetic than SAT crazed. The kid who knows not only the name of the principal but also the name of the janitor. The kid who cares about politeness over prestige. The kid who bothers to save the frog.

Being smart is valued. But being decent is *impressive*. We should inspire our kids to be both straight A students and "the nicest kid in the class." It will be wonderful if they can be both. But it only matters if they are the latter.

Works Consulted

Various sources proved to be valuable during the writing of this book. Two sources are particularly noteworthy:

1. Dartmouth admissions statistics are provided in the Dartmouth College Fact Book, published online by the Office of Institutional Research. This resource serves to make public many relevant categories and subcategories of undergraduate admissions data. (http://www.dartmouth.edu/oir/pdfs /admissions.pdf)

2. I refer to the Common Application frequently in this book. The Common Application website and applicant portal were important references. (www.commonapp.com)

Other works to note:

Anderson, Greta. "More SAT Test Takers but Lower Scores." *Inside Higher Ed*, September 24, 2019. https://www.insidehighered.com /admissions/article/2019/09/24/minority-and-first-generation-sat -scores-fall-behind.

Astin, Alexander, Kenneth Green, William Korn, and Marilynn Schalit. "The American Freshman: National Norms for Fall 1985." Los Angeles: Higher Education Research Institute, UCLA, 1985. https://www.heri.ucla.edu/PDFs/pubs/TFS/Norms/Monographs /TheAmericanFreshman1985.pdf.

Boyington, Briana. "Diversity Fly-in Programs Make Campus Visits Accessible." *U.S. News & World Report*, May 2017. https://www.usnews.com/education/best-colleges/articles/2017-05-01/diversity-fly-in-programs-make-campus-visits-accessible.

Bruni, Frank. *Where You Go Is Not Who You'll Be: An Antidote to the College Admissions Mania*. New York: Grand Central Publishing, 2015.

Centers for Disease Control and Prevention. "Data and Statistics on Children's Mental Health," March 30, 2020. https://www.cdc.gov/childrensmentalhealth/data.html.

Chetty, Raj, John Friedman, Emmanuel Saez, Nicholas Turner, and Danny Yagan. "Mobility Report Cards: The Role of Colleges in Intergenerational Mobility." NBER Working Paper 23618, National Bureau of Economic Research, Cambridge, MA, July 2017. https://doi.org/10.3386/w23618.

"Coalition for College." Accessed December 15, 2019. https://www.coalitionforcollegeaccess.org/.

Collins, Jim. "End of an Era?" *Dartmouth Alumni Magazine*, March–April 2020.

Dale, Stacy Berg, and Alan B. Krueger. "Estimating the Payoff to Attending a More Selective College: An Application of Selection on Observables and Unobservables." NBER Working Paper No. 7322, National Bureau of Economic Research, Cambridge, MA, August 1999. http://www.nber.org/papers/w7322.

Dartmouth Admissions Ambassador Program. "Conducting the Interview." Accessed April 1, 2019. http://dartmouth.imodules.com/s/1353/directory/index.aspx?sid=1353&gid=350&pgid=11126.

Dartmouth Undergraduate Admissions. "Alumni Interview." Accessed February 16, 2019. https://admissions.dartmouth.edu/glossary -term/alumni-interview.

———. "International Students." Accessed March 3, 2020. https:// admissions.dartmouth.edu/glossary-term/international-students.

Deresiewicz, William. *Excellent Sheep: The Miseducation of the American Elite and the Way to a Meaningful Life.* New York: Free Press, 2014.

DeSilver, Drew. "A Majority of U.S. Colleges Admit Most Students Who Apply." Pew Research Center, April 9, 2019. https://www .pewresearch.org/fact-tank/2019/04/09/a-majority-of-u-s-colleges -admit-most-students-who-apply/.

de Vise, Daniel. "On Common App, Georgetown Now Stands Alone." *Washington Post*, June 10, 2011. https://www.washingtonpost.com /blogs/college-inc/post/on-common-app-georgetown-now-stands -alone/2011/06/10/AGDLY4OH_blog.html.

Dixon-Román, Ezekiel J., John J. McArdle, and Howard T. Everson. "Race, Poverty and SAT Scores: Modeling the Influences of Family Income on Black and White High School Students' SAT Performance." *Teachers College Record* 115, no. 4 (May 2013). https://www.researchgate.net/publication/280232788 _Race_Poverty_and_SAT_Scores_Modeling_the_Influences _of_Family_Income_on_Black_and_White_High_School _Students'_SAT_Performance.

Eagan, Kevin, Ellen Bara Stolzenberg, Hilary B. Zimmerman, Melissa C. Aragon, Hannah Whang Sayson, and Cecelia Rios-Aguilar. "The American Freshman: National Norms Fall 2016." Los Angeles:

Higher Education Research Institute, UCLA, 2017. https://www
.heri.ucla.edu/monographs/TheAmericanFreshman2016.pdf.

Eide, Eric R., and Michael J. Hilmer. "Do Elite Colleges Lead to
Higher Salaries? Only for Some Professions." *Wall Street Journal*,
February 1, 2016. https://www.wsj.com/articles/do-elite-colleges
-lead-to-higher-salaries-only-for-some-professions-1454295674.

Eide, Eric R., Michael J. Hilmer, and Mark H. Showalter. "Is It
Where You Go or What You Study? The Relative Influence of
College Selectivity and College Major on Earnings." *Contemporary
Economic Policy* 34, no. 1 (2015): 37–46. https://doi.org/10.1111
/coep.12115.

Fiske, Edward. *Fiske Guide to Colleges 2020*. Naperville, IL:
Sourcebooks, 2019.

Furlong, Lisa. "Nuanced Decisions." *Dartmouth Alumni Magazine*,
May–June 2011.

Ge, Suqin, Elliott Isaac, and Amalia R. Miller. "Elite Schools and
Opting In: Effects of College Selectivity on Career and Family
Outcomes." SSRN, August 5, 2019. https://ssrn.com/abstract
=3284635.

Golden, Daniel. *The Price of Admission*. New York: Crown, 2006.

Hess, Abigail. "Rich Students Get Better SAT Scores—Here's Why."
CNBC, October 3, 2019. https://www.cnbc.com/2019/10/03/rich
-students-get-better-sat-scores-heres-why.html.

Ingraham, Christopher. "This Chart Shows How Much More Ivy
League Grads Make than You." *Washington Post*, September 14,

2015. http://www.washingtonpost.com/news/wonk/wp/2015/09
/14/this-chart-shows-why-parents-push-their-kids-so-hard-to-get
-into-ivy-league-schools.

Ivy League. "Prospective Athlete Information." Accessed November
1, 2019. https://ivyleague.com/sports/2017/7/28/information-psa
-index.aspx.

Jack, Anthony Abraham. *The Privileged Poor: How Elite Colleges
Are Failing Disadvantaged Students*. Cambridge, MA: Harvard
University Press, 2019.

Jaschik, Scott. "Popularity of Early Decision Continues to Grow."
Inside Higher Ed, January 7, 2019. https://www.insidehighered
.com/admissions/article/2019/01/07/popularity-early-decision
-continues-grow.

Mathews, Jay. "For Women Who Attend Elite Colleges, Pay and
Marriage Have Ups and Downs." *Washington Post*, December
28, 2018. https://www.washingtonpost.com/local/education
/for-women-who-attend-elite-colleges-pay-and-marriage
-have-ups-and-downs/2018/12/27/590f16a2-099a-11e9-88e3
-989a3e456820_story.html.

McCarthy, Claire. "Anxiety in Teens Is Rising: What's Going On?"
HealthyChildren.org. American Academy of Pediatrics, November
20, 2019. https://www.healthychildren.org/English/health-issues
/conditions/emotional-problems/Pages/Anxiety-Disorders.aspx.

Morse, Robert, and Eric Brooks. "A More Detailed Look at the
Ranking Factors." *U.S. News & World Report*, September 8, 2019.
Accessed March 5, 2020. https://www.usnews.com/education/best
-colleges/articles/ranking-criteria-and-weights.

National Center for Education Statistics. "Fast Facts: Public and Private School Comparison." National Center for Education Statistics (NCES) Home Page, a part of the U.S. Department of Education. Accessed February 21, 2020. https://nces.ed.gov/fastfacts/display .asp?id=55.

Sax, Linda, Jennifer Lindholm, Alexander Astin, William Korn, and Kathryn Mahoney. "The American Freshman: National Norms for Fall 2001." Los Angeles: Higher Education Research Institute, UCLA, 2001. https://www.heri.ucla.edu/PDFs/pubs/TFS/Norms /Monographs/TheAmericanFreshman2001.pdf.

Steinberg, Jacques. *The Gatekeepers: Inside the Admissions Process of a Premier College*. New York: Penguin Books, 2002.

Stolzenberg, Ellen Bara. "The Mental and Physical Well-Being of Incoming Freshmen: Three Decades of Research." *Higher Education Today*, February 5, 2019. https://www.higheredtoday.org/2018 /09/06/mental-physical-well-incoming-freshmen-three-decades -research/.

Thompson, Derek. "The Myth of American Universities as Inequality- Fighters." *Atlantic*, August 31, 2017. https://www.theatlantic.com /business/archive/2017/08/universities-inequality-fighters/538566/.

U.S. News & World Report. "Best College Rankings and Lists." Accessed January 1, 2019. https://www.usnews.com/best-colleges /rankings.

Weissbourd, Richard, with Trisha Ross Anderson, Brennan Barnard, Alison Cashin, and Alexis Ditkowsky. "Turning the Tide II: How Parents and High Schools Can Cultivate Ethical Character and Reduce Distress in the College Admissions Process." Making

Caring Common Project, Harvard Graduate School of Education, March 2019. https://mcc.gse.harvard.edu/reports/turning-the-tide -2-parents-high-schools-college-admissions.

Zhang, Emily. "Legacy Admissions Has a Complicated History at Selective Schools." *Dartmouth*, February 2020.

Acknowledgments

I'm deeply grateful to the many admissions colleagues, deans, Dartmouth community members, college counselors, writing mentors, friends, family, prospective students, and parents who have both inspired and encouraged the creation of *Valedictorians at the Gate*. Each has received a handwritten thank-you card.

There is no thank-you card expressive enough for Joy Tutela, James Melia, Amy Einhorn, Molly Gentine, and Jamal Sabky, who helped turn an op-ed into a hardcover. You five are truly the "best in class" and I feel so blessed to have had your support.

Lastly, I'd like to acknowledge my children, Rudy and Polly, who will someday read this book and (hopefully) hold their mom accountable for her words. I love you, regardless of résumé, rank, or runny noses. Now, go learn your A, B, Cs.

About the Author

Becky Munsterer Sabky is a former director of international admissions at Dartmouth College. She's a graduate of Colby College and received her master of arts in liberal studies degree in creative writing from Dartmouth. In addition to being an award-winning newspaper columnist, she's also the author of The Little Rippers, a children's book series about skiing. She lives in Vermont with her husband, two young children, and a lovably stubborn Labrador retriever. For more on Sabky, please visit https://beckysabky.com.